God's Principles to Matrimony

Doing it God's Way

By Jo Ann Blackmon

God's Principles to Matrimony Doing it God's Way: Understanding God's Way to Matrimony for Christian Singles who desire marriage.

Published By: J A Blackmon Word Publishing, LLC
P.O. Box 680484
Houston, TX 77268
info@jabwordpublishing.com

First Edit by Vanessa Hunter
Layout and Copyedit by Rachel Sinclaire Sparkman (Carr)
Book Cover Designed by Owais Ashraf
Makeup by Mayumi Professional Makeup Artist
Author's Photo by Heavenly Moment's Photography

ISBN: 979-8-234-06677-0

Printed in the United States of America

God's Principles to Matrimony

Doing It God's Way

Understanding God's way to matrimony for Christian singles who desire marriage

By Jo Ann Blackmon

Contents

Introduction

Some years ago, particularly after one of my personal relationships ended, I went on this quest to find out why people do what they do, specifically men, which led me to study psychology. I continued to have broken relationships with men, and I wanted to understand why. Foregoing two marriages ending in divorce, I received the revelation of God's Principles to Matrimony, Doing it God's Way. The preposition "to" is intentional, denoting a movement toward marriage.

I am a Holy Ghost-filled, Spirit-led minister and teacher who operates in the gift of prophetic teaching. The foundation for the teaching in this book is the Word of God, the King James Version (KJV), along with my personal struggles of wanting to be married. This book is written to single Christian women with a desire to marry. This book is divided into three sections, each with study scriptures to meditate on after each chapter. In the first section are four Godly Principles to Matrimony Doing it God's Way, which will lay the foundation for a Godly marriage. In the second section is the Betrothal or Engagement stage. And in the third section is what every single Christian woman is waiting and wanting for: the Marriage Covenant relationship.

SECTION 1
PREPARATION

Chapter 1
Salvation

In doing it God's way, Salvation is the very first and important godly principle to matrimony. It is the foundation upon which a godly marriage is built. Many of us may have tried to use sex as the foundation to build a marriage upon, but sex does not work. For the most part, a person can get casual sex anywhere. Building a marriage upon sex is comparable to the metaphor in Matthew 7 about building a house upon sand, which did not withstand the storms and the wind that blew against it. Most single Christian women, we have had sex before the marriage, if the relationship even got that far. Did you know that a fornicator is put in the same category as the unrighteous?

We are to walk in the Spirit, and not fulfill the lust of the flesh. We are to feed our spirit man with the proper nourishment if we want to grow and be strong in God's might. We have to guard our eye gate, ear gate, mouth gate, what we touch, what we allow to touch us, and our nose gate. We cannot watch any and every thing on television/social media and expect our spiritual sight to stay on point.

> *Know ye not that the unrighteous shall not inherit the kingdom of God? Be not deceived: neither fornicators, nor idolaters, nor adulterers, nor effeminate, nor abusers of themselves with mankind.*
> *1 Corinthians 6:9 (KJV)*

We cannot listen to negative or toxic communication on a continuously and expect to hear clearly what the Spirit is saying to us. Tell them that you are not a garbage disposal and that they should go dump their garbage somewhere else.

We cannot say anything we want because God hates a forward tongue (Proverbs 6). We cannot touch everything and everybody, nor can we allow everything and everybody to touch us, because unclean spirits are transferable. We have to be careful with smells as well. Smells can remind us of ungodly activities. For example, imagine a fine guy walks by and you pick up on the scent of his cologne and it reminds you of 'Jeffrey,' an old boyfriend who wore that cologne. Then the mind starts to go down memory lane, thinking, "I remember when…" We are to desire the sincere milk of the Word of God to grow by. Paul told the church at Corinth that no other foundation can be laid but the foundation of Jesus Christ.

> *According to the grace of God which is given unto me, as a wise masterbuilder, I have laid the foundation, and another buildeth thereon. But let every man take heed how he buildeth thereupon. For other foundation can no man lay than that is laid, which is Jesus Christ.*
> *1 Corinthians 3:10–11 (KJV)*

What is salvation? The word itself is Latin. Moreover, salvation in Hebrew is *Yeshua* or Joshua, which means, "Yah saves". Salvation is the door to the Kingdom of God. According to John 10:9, Jesus said, "I am the door: by me if any man enter in, he shall be saved, and shall go in and out, and find pasture."

Now, once we enter the Kingdom, we must start the process of becoming like Christ, because we were created in His image and likeness. We are to be an earthen vessel whereby Christ can manifest Himself through our lives as water flows through a conduit. Then we become like that tree planted by the rivers of water that brings forth fruit, and out of our bellies shall flow rivers of living water (Psalm 1:3).

We must allow God through the Holy Spirit to change our character. As the scripture says, "A man's gift maketh room for him, and bringeth him before great men" (Proverbs 18:16). Once we are before great men, it's our character that is tested. We must stay the course with God. This is where some will argue and challenge you, saying that is works and we don't have to work for salvation. Amen, that is correct, we do not have to work for salvation. Jesus paid the price of redemption for us to set us free from the wrath and penalty of sin and reconciled us back to God by the shedding of His blood so that we might have eternal life through Him. So, if we want to be transformed into His likeness, we will have to go through the transforming (metamorphosis) process. We accomplish transformation by doing what the scripture says, "be not conformed to this world: but be ye transformed by the renewing of your mind, that ye may prove what is that good, and acceptable, and perfect, will of God" (Romans 12:2, KJV). At this point, we are in the Kingdom of God, meaning we have accepted Jesus Christ as our Lord and Savior, which is called being born again.

> *For by grace are ye saved through faith; and that not of yourselves: it is the gift of God: Not of works, lest any man should boast. For we are his workmanship, created in Christ Jesus unto good works, which God hath before ordained that we should walk in them.*
> *Ephesians 2:8–10 (KJV)*

Have you ever asked yourself why things were the same

after you walked to the altar to give your life to Christ? I know for me, my thinking, actions, and behavior were the same. The question becomes, then, how could I remain the same and be born again? Nicodemus asked Jesus, how can a man be born again when he is old? Can he enter the second time into his mother's womb, and be born? Jesus said, "Verily, verily, I say unto thee, except a man be born again of water and of the Spirit, he cannot enter into the king-

> *Therefore if any man be in Christ, he is a new creature: old things are passed away; behold, all things are become new.*
> *2 Corinthians 5:17 (KJV)*

dom of God. That which is born of the flesh is flesh; and that which is born of the Spirit is spirit" (John 3:5–6, KJV). We must be baptized in water and of the Spirit. Then the Spirit can work with our soul to allow Jesus Christ to become Lord in our lives.

See, we are to become new. Not just by believing we are new! "Even so faith, if it hath not works is dead, being alone" (James 2:17, KJV). So you may ask, how do we become new? I am so glad you asked. You may have heard about Jesus' first sermon in the book of Matthew, known as the Beatitudes, a.k.a. the Sermon on the Mount. First, allow me to give you a little background leading up to Jesus teaching on the Beatitudes.

John the Baptist, who was the forerunner for Jesus, was a voice crying out in the wilderness, announcing the coming of the Messiah. Saying, "Repent ye: for the kingdom of heaven is at hand" (Matthew 3:2, KJV). See, the awaited Messiah was at hand to set up His Kingdom, like the prophet Isaiah said. We know government as a system by which a nation, a state, a community, or a church is governed, regulated, or controlled by. So, in this case it is the Kingdom of Heaven. The Kingdom of Heaven is the government that governs the Kingdom of God. Jesus the Messiah was introducing a new system of government, which would ultimately lead to a reward. Under the old system, the reward was death, but under the new system the reward is eternal life. No longer a system of offering up goats for a sin offering and rams for a burnt offering. In the book of Matthew, Jesus went out into Galilee where He began His ministry by preaching, "Repent: for the kingdom of heaven is at hand" (Matthew 4:17).

> *For unto us a child is born, unto us a son is given: and the government shall be upon his shoulder: and his name shall be called Wonderful, Counsellor, The mighty God, The everlasting Father, The Prince of Peace. Of the increase of his government and peace there shall be no end, upon the throne of David, and upon his kingdom, to order it, and to establish it with judgment and with justice from henceforth even for ever. The zeal of the LORD of hosts will perform this."*
> *Isaiah 9:6–7 (KJV)*

Jesus went throughout Galilee healing people with all types of sickness and disease. The word spread quickly throughout the land and the people went seeking Him in multitudes, where they found Him on a mountain. In the scriptures, mountains oftentimes represented or were associated with places of worship, receiving revelations and or receiving instructions from God. Jesus went up on the mountain, sat down, and when His disciples came to Him then He opened His mouth and taught the Beatitudes. This is the attitude you should be of in my Kingdom. So much in life is determined by our attitude. It may take some effort to change a bad attitude, but that change will take you farther. In any case, the word Beatitude means to be blessed. In Jesus teaching of the Beatitudes there was a distinct difference from when the Ten Commandments were given on Mount Sinai. Instead of giving a list of thou-shalt-nots, Jesus gave a list of things we are to become as citizens of the Kingdom.

> "Blessed are the poor in spirit: for theirs is the kingdom of heaven.
> Blessed are they that mourn: for they shall be comforted.
> Blessed are the meek: for they shall inherit the earth.
> Blessed are they which do hunger and thirst after righteousness: for they shall be filled.
> Blessed are the merciful: for they shall obtain mercy.
> Blessed are the pure in heart: for they shall see God.
> Blessed are the peacemakers: for they shall be called the children of God.
> Blessed are they which are persecuted for righteousness' sake: for theirs is the kingdom of heaven.
> Blessed are ye, when men shall revile you, and persecute you and shall say all manner of evil against you falsely, for my sake. Rejoice, and be exceedingly glad: for great is your reward in heaven: for so persecuted they the prophets who were before you."
> Matthew 5:3–12 (KJV)

Each verse of the Beatitudes speaks to who the disciple (follower) of Christ is to become, and not just a list of thou-shalt-nots. So, you might ask how one becomes. Is it a one-time event? No, it is not a one-time event. Becoming is a process (a life-long process). This process is often called dying to yourself, or dying to the flesh. So we can then become more like Christ in order for Christ to be manifested through our lives. As a disciple (follower) of Christ, we are to pick up our cross and follow Him.

Then said Jesus unto his disciples, "If any man will come after
me, let him deny himself and take up his cross, and follow me."
Matthew 16:24 (KJV)

"And he that taketh not his cross, and followeth after me, is
not worthy of me."
Matthew 10:38 (KJV)

"If any man will come after me, let him deny himself, and take
up his cross daily, and follow me."
Luke 9:23 (KJV)

"And whosoever doth not bear his cross, and come after me,
cannot be my disciple."
Luke 14:27 (KJV)

There is a cost to be a disciple (follower) of Christ. In the Acts of the Apostles or the book of Acts, Apostle Paul went about establishing churches throughout the land. In Antioch, Apostle Paul encouraged the new converts to continue in the faith. He said, "Confirming the souls of the disciples, and exhorting them to continue in the faith, and that we must through much tribulation enter into the kingdom of God" (Acts 14:22, KJV).

Apostle Paul often reminded the churches that they would suffer tribulation and to not be moved by the afflictions they would endure, because they had been appointed for such. The same goes for us today, we have also been appointed to suffer tribulations and to be afflicted for His name's sake.

Now, you can understand why the Beatitudes are so important. We are to become like Christ. We are not to be conformed to this world but to be transformed by the renewing of our minds. We are to have the mind of Christ. We are to be representatives of the Kingdom. We are to be an example for others to follow. We are to be living epistles read of men. We are to become new!

Ladies, what we have done in the past is not working. We are doing just like the Israelites did when God sent Moses to deliver them from Pharaoh, who was the ruler of Egypt who had enslaved them. Pharaoh was a hard taskmaster, having the Israelites make bricks without straw being provided to them. The Israelites had to gather their own straw when at one time the straw had been gathered for them (Exodus 5).

While the Israelites were in Egypt, they had plenty of food to eat. Even though Pharaoh was a hard taskmaster, he let the Israelites eat meat freely, and they also ate cucumbers, melons, leeks, onions, and garlic. Pharaoh represents the world system for all that is in the world: the lust of the flesh, the lust of the eyes, and the pride of life. Pharaoh had conditioned the Israelites' minds (mentally) to expect plenty of food without having to worry about if they were going to have food to eat or not. As Moses led the Israelites through the wilderness, they began to complain about what they did not have, no water and no food, and became dissatisfied with Moses. The Israelites thought Moses had taken them out to the wilderness to die and wondered if that was the case why Moses did not just leave them in Egypt to die. However, God supernaturally provided the Israelites with water to drink and manna to eat.

Further along in their journey in Numbers 11, the Israelites began lusting for meat and wanted to know who was going to give them meat to eat. They got bored with the manna God was providing them and started reminiscing, thinking back to when they were in Egypt saying, "at least we could eat all the fish we wanted," and wished they were back in Egypt. It is funny how quickly they forgot about the harsh treatment Pharaoh inflicted on them.

God, being a faithful God, kept His promise to the Israelites, even though He was displeased with them for complaining about the manna He provided for them to eat. Nevertheless, God told Moses He would provide the Israelites with meat. By this time, Moses had gotten tired and frustrated with the Israelites and questioned God as to why He gave him those rebellious and ungrateful people to lead. God, being who He is, a faithful God, raised up 70 elders and put His Spirit upon them to help Moses with the responsibility of leadership over the Israelites.

God sent a wind like a tide that blew in an enormous amount of quail as meat for the children of Israel to eat. However, just before the Israelites could chew and swallow the quail, God sent a plague just as quickly as He sent the quail and struck the Israelites down. God struck the taste out of their mouth. They did not even get a chance to enjoy the bounty of blessings. God is faithful and merciful, but He is also just.

Unfortunately, a lot of us have done the same as the Israelites. We have asked God to bless us with a husband. Because we do not know when God is going to send the husband, we get restless and start complaining. God, how long? How long must I wait? I see others getting married and they don't even serve You. But just as soon as a man shows up on the scene, we think that is our husband and our prayers have been answered. Then we give this man what belongs to God, our heart. We must remember our God is a jealous God and He will not have any other gods before Him.

> *But every man is tempted, when he is drawn away of his own lust, and enticed. Then when lust hath conceived, it bringeth forth sin: and sin, when it is finished, bringeth forth death.*
> *James 1:14–15 (KJV)*

Let me share a personal testimony with you here. I had been divorced from my first marriage for a little over 10 years and was back in church doing the church work stuff. My children had graduated from high school and I had an empty nest. I found myself lonely and bored with my life, and I desired to be touched by a man in all the wrong ways. Yes, with my saved self. I am not proud of it, but I am only sharing with hopes that my testimony will help someone or even prevent someone from doing what I did.

See, my love language was sex. I did not know how to be intimate outside of the bedroom. If I had known then what I know now, I would not have gone down that road. So, I started praying to God for a husband. I had a list of things I wanted in my husband. I wanted him to be saved with no children, and I wanted him to be a good cook, just to name a few things, but my list was long. The thought never crossed my mind that the man I was praying for had a list too. I am sure having sex before marriage was not on his list.

As time passed, I got tired of waiting. I was ready to get married again. I had not received what I was asking for because I asked amiss. So I turned back to what was familiar and pursued a man. This guy was someone I had met about five and half years prior. I knew he was attracted to me and I was attracted to him, but I was also scared he would break my heart. So, I did not allow myself to get involved with him back then when we first met.

I started thinking about how to reconnect with him. I had three tickets to a play that had just come to town. I thought why not, I would invite him to attend the play with me. So, I reached out to him by telephone and invited him to the play.

He said yes and met me there. He was single, had a good job, a nice car, dressed neatly, well-groomed, smelled good, looked good, had a nice physique, had his own home, and plenty of money. So sure enough, we started dating.

We dated for about a year and even talked about marriage, but I began to see red flags. He was a drinker of alcohol. I ignored the red flag even though I did not want to marry someone who drank. Another red flag popped up: he liked to go out to the nightclub. I ignored that red flag, knowing I did not want to be married to someone who liked to hang out in the clubs at night.

Another red flag popped up: one day when I was visiting he got a phone call from a female who wanted to borrow some money. I remember him talking to her with a harsh tone of voice while on the phone. I knew that a man would not let his money go without some type of reassurance, just in case she could not repay the borrowed money.

So, slowly my eyes began to open, because I was not totally gone, but I was on my way. We both were of different faiths. He was Baptist and I was Pentecostal. I remembered telling him that I did not want to join a Baptist church. His reply was that I could continue attending my church and he would continue going to his church. Well, that was not going to work for me. That was the straw that broke the camel's back. So, I eventually broke off the relationship.

You know, I really wanted to blame it all on the devil, but it was not the devil. It was my flesh leading me. I thank God that I did not get struck down like the complaining Israelites. But I did get judged and was chastised for not waiting on God.

God's timing is not our timing. At that time in my life, the only thing I was thinking about was becoming someone's wife. I had no other aspirations. I was not desiring to find out what my God-given purpose in life was while here on this earth. I didn't even know who I was, but yet I wanted to get married. If God had given me what I wanted, I would have lost myself in the marriage, or worse been destroyed.

Another man came along and I just knew this one must be from God because he was preaching the gospel. So, I ended up marrying him after only being acquainted with him for less than a month.

Well, that marriage did not last. Then I realized that being married to a saved man was not easy, and there were many things I was not prepared for because I lacked knowledge and understanding. For one, the Jezebel spirit.

When the Jezebel spirit showed up on the scene I did not have the understanding of how to deal with that spirit. It appeared that my husband was being seduced and welcomed it. So to him I sounded like a nagging wife. You know, that was one of the reasons why I married him, because I thought I would not have to be concerned with unfaithfulness since he was in the church. But I had enough sense to know that when a man allows himself to be influenced by another woman to the point where he puts her above his wife, saved or not, that's a problem!

I tried to stay in the marriage, but that marriage was just an accident waiting to happen. I believe God used that marriage to increase my understanding and to prepare me to become the wife He has called me to be to the man who is looking for his good thing. It was ironic to me that the Jezebel spirit showed up on the scene in both my marriages.

In my first marriage, I did not have a name for it other than cheating. We have to learn how to deal with the Jezebel spirit, because anywhere there is authority, she or he wants to lead from behind the scenes. Jezebel is a spirit and can be in a man or woman. The Jezebel spirit is always looking for the Ahab spirit to partner up with, especially if the Jezebel spirit is working through a woman.

In 1 Kings 16–22, a woman named Jezebel married Ahab, a king of Samaria, who was a wicked and weak king. King Ahab wanted to buy Naboth's vineyard, but Naboth refused to sell it to him. King Ahab really wanted Naboth's vineyard because it was close to his palace. King Ahab became depressed and Jezebel saw it. Jezebel told King Ahab don't worry, "I will get it for you." The spirit of Jezebel is looking for those in authority who are willing to lay down their authority or who are afraid to use their authority.

For instance, Barak, an Israelite warrior. When God called Barak to attack Sisera, he was afraid to go. Deborah, who was a judge and prophetess in the book of Judges, was the one who told Barak what God was calling him to do. Barak told

Deborah, "If you will go with me, I will go; if not I will not go."

So, we must learn about demonic spirits and how they will try to work against the marriage and everything God has given us. The weapons will form against us, but they will not prosper unless we give up or give in.

Personal scriptures to meditate on:

•   Romans 1:16 – For I am not ashamed of the gospel of Christ: for it is the power of God unto salvation to every one that believeth.

•   Hebrews 4:12 – For the word of God is quick, and powerful, and sharper than any twoedged sword, piercing even to the dividing asunder of soul and spirit, and of the joints and marrow, and is a discerner of the thoughts and intents of the heart.

•   Psalm 119:130 – The entrance of thy words giveth light; it giveth understanding unto the simple.

•   2 Timothy 3:15 – The holy scriptures, which are able to make thee wise unto salvation through faith which is in Christ Jesus.

•   Exodus 14:13 – And Moses said unto the people, "Fear ye not, stand still, and see the salvation of the LORD, which He will shew to you."

- Psalm 119:105 – Thy word is a lamp unto my feet, and a light unto my path.

- Romans 10:17 – So then faith cometh by hearing, and hearing by the word of God.

- James 1:22 – But be ye doers of the word, and not hearers only, deceiving your own selves.

- 1 Peter 1:23 – Being born again, not of corruptible seed, but of incorruptible, by the word of God, which liveth and abideth for ever.

- Acts 20:32 – And now, brethren, I commend you to God, and to the word of his grace, which is able to build you up, and to give you an inheritance among all them which are sanctified.

Chapter 2
Purity

Purity is the second most important godly principle of matrimony. *Purity* is defined as freedom from adulteration or contamination; freedom from immorality, especially of a sexual nature. *Sanctification* is defined as sanctify; set apart as or declare holy; consecrate. *Purification* is defined as the process of extracting something from a substance; the process of making something spiritually or ceremonially clean.

Purification and sanctification go hand in hand. Sanctification begins with asking for forgiveness. If we confess our sins, God is faithful and just to forgive us of all unrighteousness.

After King David sinned with Bathsheba by impregnating her, he sent Bathsheba's husband, one of his soldiers, to the front line to be killed trying to cover his sin (2 Samuel 11–12). King David prayed, asking the Lord to have mercy on him, blot out his transgressions, and cleanse him from his sin. Sanctification is being washed by the water of the word. King David asked God to purge him with hyssop, so that he might be clean, to wash him so that he might be whiter than snow. King David realized that he could not clean himself just like we cannot clean ourselves in our own strength.

Under the Mosaic Law, there were three rituals used for purification: one for leprosy, one for sexual discharges, and one for contact with a dead body. When the plague of leprosy was found in a man, he had to be taken to the priest to determine whether he was clean or unclean. If the priest saw that the rising skin was white, and the hair had turned white, and raw flesh was visible, the priest would pronounce the man unclean because the raw flesh was leprosy.

The priest used two clean live birds, cedar wood, scarlet, and hyssop for the cleansing process. One of the birds would be killed in an earthen vessel over running water, and then the priest would take the living bird, the cedar wood, scarlet and the hyssop, dip them in the blood of the bird that was killed and sprinkle it upon the man to be cleansed from leprosy seven times, and then pronounce the man clean.

The number seven symbolizes completion and is frequently used in the Bible. Once the live bird was dipped seven times, the bird was released, representing the releasing of the scapegoat, like in the Day of Atonement ritual for those who had sinned. Regarding the sexual discharge ritual, the Bible refers to sexual discharge as a running issue out of the flesh to be unclean (i.e., discharge from a male's genitals and blood from a woman's genitals).

Whenever the running issue cleared up, they would wait for seven days and on the eighth day they would take two turtles

> *Thus shall ye separate the children of Israel from their uncleanness; that they die not in their uncleanness, when they defile my tabernacle that is among them. This is the law of him that hath an issue, and of him whose seed goeth from him, and is defiled therewith; And of her that is sick of her flowers, and of him that hath an issue, of the man, and of the woman, and of him that lieth with her that is unclean.*
>
> *Leviticus 15:31–33 (KJV)*

or two young pigeons to the priest. The priest would offer one of the pigeons for a sin offering, and the other one for a burnt offering, and the priest would make an atonement before the Lord for the issue of uncleanness.

Those who made contact with a dead body would be considered unclean as well. The unclean person would have to then leave the camp behind for seven days before they would be considered clean again. The ritual for impurity from exposure to a dead body required a sin offering on the third and seventh day and that would render the unclean person clean.

I am reminded of the women who had the issue of blood for 12 years, who touched the hem of Jesus garment, and was healed or made whole immediately. We no longer have to go to a priest to get clean. Jesus Christ is our High Priest now and we can go to Him by prayer and supplication with thanksgiving and make our request known.

After Apostle Paul heard news from the Corinthian church that, when gathered together for Holy Communion, some members were gathering for the wrong reason, which caused division among their congregation (1 Corinthians 11:17–34). Paul dealt with the Corinthian church about proper worship.

He said some members were partaking of the Lord's Supper because they were hungry, and some because they were drunk. Paul explained to the Corinthian church that because some members had partaken of the Lord's Supper without examining themselves, they were unworthy and brought damnation to themselves.

Paul also explained to the Corinthian church that this was the reason why many among them were weak, sickly, and many had died, because they did not discern the Lord's body.

See, fornication is one of those sins that is against our own body, meaning the results of the sin will manifest in the body. That is a reason why so many among the body of Christ are weak, sickly, and many have died due to sinning against their own body and did not ask the Lord for forgiveness before taking the Lord's Supper.

Remember, the believer has been set apart for the Master's use. The Bible tells us that the body is the temple of God, in which God's Spirit dwells. We have been bought with a price, and we are no longer our own.

I asked the Lord how He dwells in us. He likens it to the tabernacle of the Mosaic Law. Under the dispensation of Law, the tabernacle was so important during that time because it was where the presence of God dwelt in the Holy of Holies. After the priest had washed in the brazen laver, the wash pot, to prepare himself to go into the Holy of Holies to atone for his sins and the sins of the people. That ritual was done away with at the coming of Jesus Christ.

Now we are under the dispensation of Grace, we are the tabernacle that houses God's Spirit. We have been chosen as royal priests or as a royal priesthood and a Holy nation and we are to minister praise to God who has called us out of darkness and into His marvelous light. Meaning we can now go before the throne of God boldly for ourselves.

Keep in remembrance that God's Spirit will not dwell in an unclean temple. Under the Law, if the priest had gone into the Holy of Holies unclean, he would have died inside. Today, our sins separate us from God, which causes us to die spiritually or to become spiritually dead. In comparison to the three parts of the tabernacle the outer court, the inner court, and the Holy of Holies, we are a three part being. We have a spirit and we have a soul. Both the spirit and soul lives within the body.

Our body is a type of the outer court which will return back to dirt and will not enter into heaven. Our soul is made up of our mind, our will, our emotions, and our spirit. And it is our spirit that is quickened or made alive to God.

The devil is after our soul, and if he cannot get our soul, he will go after the body, but we are not to fear the one who can kill the body, but fear the one who can kill both the body and the soul.

Our soul is the core of man. That is the part of us we are to renew, we are to work out our own soul salvation with fear and trembling by the renewing of the mind. Our unsaved soul is the wide gate leading us to destruction. There must be a purging of the soul; in other words, we must be delivered from the strongholds of wickedness, envy, strife, jealousy, witchcraft, lying, hate, uncleanliness, fornication, drunkenness, just to name a few. These things are works of the flesh in which the strongman will use to his advantage to cause us to walk in disobedience like he did with Eve in the garden. Plus, the works of the flesh will cause us to not inherit the Kingdom of God.

> *Ye are of God, little children, and have overcome them: because greater is He that is in you, than he that is in the world.*
> *1 John 4:4 (KJV)*

God has given the church Deliverance Ministers who can assist His people with getting delivered from the strongman who is trying to work through our souls. I know what you are thinking, you are thinking that a Christian cannot be possessed with a demon. That is correct, because the house is filled already with the Spirit of God. However, a Christian's soul can be oppressed, depressed, and influenced by the activities of a demon.

We are to seek after and develop the fruit of the Spirit in our lives which are love: the God kind of love, agape; joy: the joy of the Lord is our strength; peace: the peace that God gives that surpasseth all our understanding; longsuffering, which will work patience in us: let patience have her perfect work; gentleness: a soft answer turns away wrath; we are to have faith: without faith it is impossible to please God; we are to be meek: the meek will inherit the earth; we are to have temperance: control our temper, be swift to hear and slow to speak, slow to wrath: the wrath of man does not work the righteousness of God.

We who are of Christ have crucified the affections and lusts of our flesh. If we live by the Spirit we will walk in the Spirit. We cannot just claim sanctification in name only. Sanctification is a process by which we are becoming more like Christ.

In the parable of the fig tree (Luke 13:6–9), "A certain man had a fig tree planted in his vineyard; and he came and sought fruit thereon, and found none. Then said he unto the dresser of his vineyard, Behold, these three years, I come seeking fruit on this fig tree, and find none: cut it down; why cumbereth it the ground?" The fig tree might have looked liked it should have figs on

> *Not that which goeth into the mouth defileth a man; but that which cometh out of the mouth, this defileth a man.*
> *Matthew 15:11 (KJV)*

it, but did not and no one was able to eat from it.

We don't want to be like that fig tree, looking like a Christian on the outside, but inward we are barren possessing no fruit. Having a form of godliness, but denying the power of God. In Christ's eyesight, we become useless and good for nothing but to be cast out and to be trodden under by the foot of men.

I can testify of this in my own life. In my second marriage, I was married to a narcissist, but at that time I was not aware of it. I had done every thing I knew to do to try to please my husband during that time, but nothing was ever right or good enough. Something was always either too long or too short. If he gave me a compliment, he would cancel it out by saying something negative, trying to tear me down and break my spirit. He rarely said 'thank you' to me. He had a sense of entitlement to whatever I was doing for him like I was supposed to do those things for him. I would tell him what I did for him was because I wanted to do them and not because I was being made to do them or even had to do them. He did not understand that.

> *For whosoever will save his life shall lose it: and whosoever will lose his life for my sake shall find it. For what is a man profited, if he shall gain the whole world, and loses his own soul? or what shall a man give in exchange for his soul?*
> *Matthew 16:25–26 (KJV)*

When I finally came to my senses and realized that demonic activities were at work through him trying to bring my soul into captivity, I stopped trying to please him. Whenever demonic activity shows up on the scene, it comes only to steal, kill, and destroy. The devil is not trying to celebrate us.

I prayed to God asking for forgiveness, and I asked for a way out of the marriage. I am not trying to paint a picture that makes my second husband look like the villain, because it was not all his fault. I played a major part in the demise of my second marriage by being disobedient to God. I was yet immature in the area of relationships and inexperienced with men. I put myself and my desires before the truth of God's Word.

Satan meant it for evil but God turned it around and made it for His good pleasure. Thank God, I had enough sense to know I was worth more than what I was receiving. God allowed me to go through those indignations in my marriage because that was my chastisement for not doing it His way and for not waiting on Him to move in my life concerning marriage.

As we strive for purity, we are being freed from evil and wickedness and we are to be refined as pure gold. Living a pure life consists of having a mind focused on not allowing sin to dictate our decisions. The streets of heaven are paved with pure gold because who may stand in His holy place is the one who has clean hands and a pure heart.

My daily prayer to the Lord is to create in me a clean heart and renew a right spirit within me and to wash me whiter than snow. We must resist the devil and submit to God and the devil will flee for a season. He will be back in a different person, but it is the same evil spirit trying to deceive God's people. We have to be on alert, watch as well as pray.

We have to get to the point in our lives that we no longer want to be just someone's sex object or play toy, because we have more to offer than just sex. We have a mind, creativity, and abilities galore. I had gotten to the point in my marriage where I did not like sex any more. Sex made me feel dirty, but that was part of my process. A marriage without affection is a bedroom without respect and compassion—Just roll over and give me sex like you are some kind of freak. I had to learn how to live a pure life. For me, I have found it hard to find even a saved man who does not have sex on their mind.

> Keep thy heart with all diligence; for out of it are the issues of life. Put away from thee a froward mouth, and perverse lips put far from thee. Proverbs 4:23–24 (KJV)

Sex is one of man's weaknesses, and the Jezebel spirit knows that. Some saved men like to flirt around with sex, and that is one way another woman can wreak havoc in a home because the man is being seduced.

Marriage is ordained by God, and He said that it is not good for man to be alone, that means women too. Two is better than one. A person can put to flight a thousand and two ten thousand. So, in His timing, marriage will happen for me again, and for you. But until then, God is preparing us for the responsibility (burden) of marriage.

I am reminded of the lukewarm church of Laodicea. They were known for their works, but they were neither cold nor hot. God wished that they be one or the other, but not both. But because they were lukewarm and neither cold nor hot, God spewed them out of His mouth. He could not trust them to carry out His perfect will.

We are to be wise as a serpent but harmless as a dove. We are to be on fire for the Lord. We are to be like that gold in the refiner's fire until the impurities rise to the surface so we can get rid of the impurities. The heart is wicked, who can know it? That is why we need a pure heart, a heart that fears God.

The fear of God is the beginning of wisdom. Most people do

not think they need deliverance from the works of the flesh, because they have always been a certain way or have always thought a certain way. So, the devil, being cunning and deceitful, has merged himself in with our personalities.

The person who doesn't know a wicked spirit—Jezebel, who is controlling, dominating, and manipulative—has attached itself to their personality, or some other strongman has attached itself to their personality, is in trouble. The Jezebel spirit seeks those who are in some type of leadership role, whether it be in the home, church, or on the job. The Jezebel spirit wants to be worshiped and in control.

I am reminded of when the devil tempted Jesus, he took Him up on a high mountain and showed Jesus all the kingdoms of the world. Yes, the devil has a kingdom too, and it is the kingdom of darkness. The devil told Jesus to look at all this power and glory he would give to Him if He would worship him. Now you know if the devil tempted Jesus, he is going to tempt us.

> Remember the word that I said unto you, The servant
> is not greater than his lord. If they have persecuted me,
> they will also persecute you; if they have kept my saying,
> they will keep yours also.
> John 15:20 (KJV)

Personal scriptures to meditate on:

- 1 Timothy 4:12 – Let no man despise thy youth; but be thou an example of the believers, in word, in conversation, in charity, in spirit, in faith, in purity.

- 1 Corinthians 6:18 – Flee fornication. Every sin that a man doeth is without the body; but he that committeth fornication sinneth against his own body.

- 1 Corinthians 3:16 – Know ye not that ye are the temple of God, and that the Spirit of God dwelleth in you?

- 1 Corinthians 6:13 – Meats for the belly, and the belly for meats: but God shall destroy both it and them. Now the body is not for fornication, but for the Lord; and the Lord for the body.

- 1 Thessalonians 4:7 – For God hath not called us unto uncleanness, but unto holiness.

- 1 Timothy 5:22 – Lay hands suddenly on no man, neither be partaker of other men's sins: keep thyself pure.

- James 4:8 – Draw nigh to God, and he will draw nigh to you. Cleanse your hands, ye sinners; and purify your hearts, ye double minded.

- James 3:17 – But the wisdom that is from above is first pure, then peaceable, gentle, and easy to be intreated, full of mercy and good fruits, without partiality and without hypocrisy.

- Galatians 5:17 – For the flesh lusteth against the Spirit, and the Spirit against the flesh: and these are contrary the one to the another: so that ye cannot do the things that ye would.

- Philippians 4:8 – Finally, brethren, whatsoever things are true, whatsoever things are honest, whatsoever things are just, whatsoever things are pure, whatsoever things are lovely, whatsoever things are of a good report; if there be any virtue, and if there be any praise, think on these things.

- 1 Corinthians 10:13 – There hath no temptation taken you but such as is common to man: but God is faithful, who will not suffer you to be tempted above that ye are able; but will with the temptation also make a way to escape, that ye may be able to bear it.

- 1 Corinthians 7:1b – It is good for a man not to touch a woman.

- 1 Corinthians 6:12 – All things are lawful unto me, but all things are not expedient: all things are lawful for me, but I will not be brought under the power of any.

- 1 Thessalonians 4:3–4 – For this is the will of God, even your sanctification, that ye should abstain from fornication. That every one of you should know how to possess his vessel in sanctification and honour.

- 1 Corinthians 6:15 – Know ye not that your bodies are the members of Christ? Shall I then take the members of Christ, and make them the members of an harlot? God forbid.

- Proverbs 31:10 – Who can find a virtuous woman? For her price is far above rubies.

- James 1:12 – Blessed is the man that endureth temptation: for when he is tried, he shall receive the crown of life, which the Lord hath promised to them that love him.

- 1 John 1:9 – If we confess our sins, he is faithful and just to forgive us our sins, and to cleanse us from all unrighteousness.

Chapter 3
The Kingdom

Seeking the Kingdom is the third most important godly principle to matrimony. After Jesus taught on the Beatitudes, He told his disciples (followers) not to worry about their life, what they were going to eat, or drink, or wear, but to seek the Kingdom first.

As part of my personal journey, I read Matthew 6:33 and quoted it many times, but I did not really have a revelation of what it meant. If I had received a revelation, I would not have been double-minded about my Christian walk. On some days, I would seek the Kingdom, but then on other days, I would seek after a husband. First of all, I was not supposed to be the hunter, and I should not have been the one seeking and chasing. Ladies, we must stop being desperate for a man/husband to be in our lives to make us feel complete.

> *But seek ye first the kingdom of God, and His righteousness; and all these things shall be added unto you. Take therefore no thought for the morrow: for the morrow shall take thought for the things of itself. Sufficient unto the day is the evil thereof.*
> *Matthew 6:33–34 (KJV)*

We are to be whole in Christ first. Desperation will cause us to become the target of a predator, one who is going to and fro seeking whom he may devour. Proverbs tells us that he who finds a wife finds a good thing and obtains favor from the Lord. The devil wants to pervert and change God's order for mankind regarding marriage.

The Bible speaks of these things in 2 Timothy 3:2–5, "For men shall be lovers of their own selves, covetous, boasters, proud, blasphemers, disobedient to parents, unthankful, unholy, without natural affection, trucebreakers, false accusers, incontinent, fierce, despisers of those that are good, traitors, heady, highminded, lovers of pleasures more than lovers of God." We have become a people of pleasure with a need to be entertained trying to fill a void, an emptiness in our hearts. Don't get me wrong, I like to enjoy the finer things of life. However, I have learned there must be a balance because a false balance is an abomination to God.

We are to remain humble and not to think more highly of ourselves then we should. We are to remind ourselves that God knows what is best for us and to trust His Word. In Maslow's hierarchy of needs theory, we are to seek "self-actualization". The only problem with seeking self-actualization is that it leaves God out and leads us to self-sufficiency. We are to acknowledge God in all our ways, lean not to our own understanding, and He will direct our path. The Word is a lamp unto our feet and a light unto our path. He will light up our pathway so we can see clearly which way to go.

I have asked God a many times to show me which way to go. It has taken me a long time to see what God has been trying to show me all these years. I, too, was like the children of Israel: When I was set free from bondage, I wandered for many years in the wilderness of my mind. But God! He knows when we are ready to receive what He has promised us. We all will have a wilderness (wandering) experience, and it is necessary for the transition from depending on Pharaoh's (world) system to depending on God's (Kingdom) system.

Due to the children of Israel's lack of faith, disobedience, and lack of trust in God, it took them 40 years to get to the Promised Land, which was only an 11-day journey. We do not want to be like the children of Israel. We want to obtain what God has predestined for us so we can leave a Godly inheritance and legacy to our children.

God knew the Israelites were not ready in their minds for the Promised Land because they still had a slave mentality, which is why they had to go through the wilderness. The Israelites got so close to Canaan that they could almost touch it, but because they believed a negative report from 10 of the spies who had gone ahead: the city of Canaan was a fortified city and looked ready to fight off any attack at any time. This negative report made the Israelites feel hopeless of ever obtaining the Promised Land.

The Israelites forgot that God said that He would give the land to them; all they had to do was go and take possession. The Israelites allowed what they saw in Canaan to strip them down to hopelessness and fear. They did not see how they were going to overtake such a well fortified city. Then they resorted to what they did best, complaining about Moses and his leadership.

They wanted to overthrow Moses and appoint another leader to take them back to Egypt. That is crazy. They would rather go back to Egypt and die there instead of trying to possess the Promised Land. Now that sounds just like a women who has been in an abusive relationship, and God finally set her free to leave and live life free from abuse. Once she is freed, she runs into some challenging situations which causes her to feel like she is in a hopeless situation. Then she begins to say to herself, when I was with him at least he paid the bills, I had a roof over my head, and I had food to eat, thinking that she was better off in the abusive relationship.

The Israelites allowed their circumstances to lead them instead of trusting in what God had said. God was trying to get the Israelites to trust and believe in His provisions for their lives. God is trying to do the same today for us. Let's not look to man or this world but let us look unto the hills from whence cometh our help. Our help comes from the Lord.

> *For since the beginning of the world men have not heard, nor perceived by the ear, neither hath the eye seen, O God, beside thee, what he hath prepared for him that waiteth for him.*
> *Isaiah 64:4 (KJV)*

We are to wait upon the Lord, for He will renew our strength. We are to seek God's righteousness, because there is none righteous. We have to get to a point in our lives that we are mature in our beliefs. Then we will grow from just believing to doing, because when we do righteousness we become righteous, as the Lord is righteous.

The Bible says that our righteousness is as filthy rags (Isaiah 64:6). The scribes and Pharisees were known to be religious leaders who interpreted and enforced the law. However, Jesus said, "That except your righteousness shall exceed the righteousness of the scribes and Pharisees, ye shall in no case enter into the kingdom of heaven" (Matthew 5:20, KJV)

Notice, Jesus did not say Kingdom of God, because the Kingdom of Heaven is what governs the Kingdom of God. As a citizen of the Kingdom, Jesus Christ is our King. He is the King of kings and Lord of lords. He is the one who is, who was, and who is to come, He is King Jesus.

As part of my personal journey, I have dealt with a lot of mental (mind) battles. The enemy was after my mind by tormenting me with the spirit of fear. I dealt with panic attacks, depression, and anxiety. When I was around 34, I accepted the call into ministry, not knowing that I had to go through a process to possess what God had for me. Actually, I was called when I was in my mother's womb, as a prophetic teacher of God's Word. Nevertheless, I was fortunate and thankful to have been under a loving leader, who allowed his young ministers to speak the Word on Sunday mornings as an opportunity to develop our gifts. But the anxiety I experienced got so overwhelming that I wanted to quit speaking in front of the people.

> *And He said unto me, My grace is sufficient for thee: for my strength is made perfect in weakness.*
> *2 Corinthians 12:9 (KJV)*

Thank God, I did not quit, because over time, I overcame the anxiety that came with speaking in front of others. I learned to confess: God has not given me the spirit of fear but of power and of love and a soundness of mind (2 Timothy 1:7). Mental illness was a generational curse that ran through my family. However, I was determined that the buck stopped with me. I did not want to pass that curse down to my children. The strategy the enemy used on me was through relationships.

Now, let me explain, I was a naïve young lady with the mindset of an innocent little girl. I had not been tarnished by the world yet and had not been taught about men and how to have a relationship with the opposite sex. So of course, the men saw that, and some took advantage of my innocence with my consent. I had not been in many relationships and was inexperienced. Moreover, what I was calling love was nothing more than infatuation. Therefore, my relationships ended badly due to outside interference.

In one instance, when one of my relationships ended, I encountered the spirit of rejection. Then I finally felt what I had been trying to avoid all my adult life, rejection. I remember when I was in kindergarten, there was a girl who picked on me and bullied me for no reason. That was my first experience with rejection, and I did not like it.

When I was in the third grade, I wanted to be liked and accepted by a popular group of girls at school. I would take extra candy to school just so I would have enough to share with them so they would play with me. It worked for a while until one of the girls figured out what I was doing, and then they stopped playing with me.

I remember another occasion when I was about 15 years old. I experienced rejection from a group of neighborhood girls. One of the girl's ex-boyfriends started to like me, and we were calling ourselves boyfriend and girlfriend, and he had given me one of his rings to wear. Apparently, his ex-girlfriend was not ready to let him go. She turned the other neighborhood girls against me. So, one day, the neighborhood girls decided they were going to ambush me and had encircled me so that I could not get away. Mind you, I had never been in a fight before in my young life, and I could just see myself getting beat down. But the Lord had a ram in the bush for me, which provided me away of escape.

A couple of young ladies just happened to be walking by at that time, and they told the group of girls to let me go. I was glad to see them, because I did not know what I was going to do. I was outnumbered. So, I ran home and did not tell a soul what just happened to me until now. I was ashamed.

From that point on, I said that I would never be in a clique again. I discovered that when you are in a clique, if you do not do or act the way they want you to, they will turn on you. I said all of that to say that God allowed me to experience rejection at an early age because He knew I would need to know how to deal with the spirit of rejection for where He was taking me in ministry.

> *He is despised and rejected of men; a man of sorrows, and acquainted with grief: and we hid as it were our faces from him; he was despised, and esteemed him not. Surely he hath borne our griefs, and carried our sorrows: yet we did esteem him stricken, smitten of God, and afflicted. But he was wounded for our transgressions, he was bruised for our iniquities: the chastisement of our peace was upon him; and with his stripes we are healed.*
> *Isaiah 53:3–5 (KJV)*

I am reminded of the story of Abraham and Issac. God told Abraham to take his only son Issac up to the mountain to offer him as a burnt offering. On their way to the place where the sacrifice was to be made, Issac asked his father, Abraham, where the lamb for the burnt offering was. Abraham told his son that God would provide a lamb. When they got there, Abraham built an altar, laid the wood, bound and laid Issac on the altar.

As Abraham got ready to slay his only son Issac, the angel of the Lord told Abraham not to slay his son, for there was a ram in the bush. I have learned to seek the Lord for direction before jumping off into a relationship, and to make sure it is all right with Him. I am looking to God through the Holy Spirit to order my steps and to lead me in the path He would have me to go.

For the kingdom of God is not meat and drink; but righteousness, and peace, and joy in the Holy Ghost.
Romans 14:17 (KJV)

Personal scriptures to meditate on:

- 1 Corinthians 4:20 – For the kingdom of God is not in word, but in power.

- Luke 12:32 – Fear not, little flock; for it is your Father's good pleasure to give you the kingdom.

- Psalm 5:12 – For thou, Lord, wilt bless the righteous; with favour wilt thou compass him as with a shield.

- Matthew 12:28 – But if I cast out devils by the Spirit of God, then the kingdom of God is come unto you.

- Luke 17:21 – Neither shall they say, Lo here! or, lo there! for, behold, the kingdom of God is within you.

- Matthew 6:10 – Thy kingdom come, Thy will be done in earth, as it is in heaven.

- Matthew 16:19 – And I will give unto thee the keys of the kingdom of heaven: and whatsoever thou shalt bind on earth shall be bound in heaven: and whatsoever thou shalt loose on earth shall be loosed in heaven.

- Luke 11:20 –But if I with the finger of God cast out devils, no doubt the kingdom of God is come upon you.

Chapter 4
Wholeness

Wholeness is the fourth most important godly principle to matrimony. Wholeness is defined as the quality of being complete or a single unit, not broken or divided into parts. After trying to do things our own way, we find ourselves broken in our souls from failed marriages, abusive relationships, disrespect, and regret. From there, we are left with a void in our hearts. God does not want burnt offerings as a sacrifice any longer. We are to present our bodies as a living sacrifice, holy and acceptable to Him. God is looking for a broken spirit and a contrite heart, because only then are we pliable. He can put us back on the potter's wheel because the clay was marred in the potter's hand.

> *O house of Israel, cannot I do with you as this potter? saith the Lord. Behold, as the clay is in the potter's hand, so are ye in mine hand, O house of Israel.*
> *Jeremiah 18:6 (KJV)*

As part of my personal journey, when I was in my thirties I avoided falling in love for a long time. I had always held back part of my heart. Remember, I was rejected from the one man I really wanted and loved. I believe that was a necessary experience and lesson for me to learn from because I had put that man ahead of everybody in my life. That experience left me in the hospital battling an emotional breakdown. But I am thankful to God, He did not allow that experience to destroy me but to make me better.

God began to open my spiritual eyes to see that what I had gone through was a spiritual attack against my mind. The devil was trying to destroy me before I would come to recognize and understand the call on my life. I began to seek God for my life, and I allowed God to work on me through the Holy Spirit, to heal my brokenheartedness through speaking the Word of God to my situation. I found scriptures that dealt with fear, joy, and peace, and I began speaking those scriptures over my life.

By Christ, the one who reconciled us back into good standing with God, has healed the separation and brokenness in us that was created by sin. Wholeness in our spirit, mind, and body is a singleness of mind where we can be at peace and rest in God. We are to take on God's yoke and learn of Him. There has to be a period of healing toward wholeness from bad relationships. For example, after a break-up (divorce) the soul needs time to heal. It is not healthy to jump back into another relationship trying to fill that void. Use that time to allow God to show you yourself and to reveal Himself to you.

God is the only one who can satisfy and fill that void in our lives. Wholeness is a place of freedom where we are no longer tossed to and fro by every wind and doctrine. Wholeness is a place of spiritual maturity where we have become stable minded. We must personalize the word of God in our confession of the scriptures.

> My flesh and my heart faileth: but God is the strength of
> my heart, and my portion for ever.
> Psalm 73:26 (KJV)

He sent his word, and healed [me], and delivered [me]
from their destructions.
Psalm 107:20 (KJV)

Why art thou cast down, O my soul? and why art thou
disquieted in me? hope thou in God: for I shall yet praise
him for the help of his countenance.
Psalm 42:5 (KJV)

See, we have to do like David, we have to talk to God and seek God for our healing and deliverance from our broken state of mind. The battleground is the mind; that is where we must fight.

When I was in the military, they trained us for battle. We had to become familiar with our weapon both inside and out; we had learn to identify the enemy's tactical vehicles; we had to endure the terrain with our gear on our backs and weapon in hand as we walked the terrain for miles; and we had to learn how to live out of tents and eat T-rations. We did all of that and more preparing for battle in the time of peace.

(For the weapons of our warfare are not carnal, but mighty through God to the pulling down of strong holds;) Casting down imaginations, and every high thing that exalteth itself against the knowledge of God, and bringing into captivity every thought to the obedience of Christ.
2 Corinthians 10:4–5 (KJV)

As believers, we do not fight a carnal war but a spiritual war called spiritual warfare. We are to prepare our minds for battle as well during the times of peace. We have to learn how to cast down imaginations and thoughts that come against the knowledge of God and come against who God says that we are in Him.

We are to guard our hearts with all diligence, and don't allow any and everything into our hearts. When negative words are spoken to us and against us, we are to grab those words and speak the Word of God to counter attack what has been spoken.

> *Put on the whole armour of God, that ye may be able to stand against the wiles of the devil. For we wrestle not against flesh and blood, but against principalities, against powers, against the rulers of the darkness of this world, against spiritual wickedness in high places.*
> Ephesians 6:11–12 (KJV)

Words spoken to us that are negative, abusive, and disrespectful come to block, hinder, or delay what God want us to know about who we are in Christ. I am reminded that the Kingdom of God suffers violence, but the violent take it by force. We have to speak the Word of God with force against what was spoken to us. In Christ, we are a force to be reckoned with.

To be whole is to be one with God in body, soul, and spirit. To have a close relationship with God where we can talk to Him and He can talk to us. Most times, we will have to get along with God in our closet or quiet place. We will have to slow our lives down from the non-essentials (noise) to hear what God is saying through the Holy Spirit to make us whole in Christ. Wholeness takes time and cannot be rushed. Wholeness is a process working together with the Holy Spirit. We must know that even though our outward man perish, our inward man is being renewed daily.

And the very God of peace sanctify you wholly;
and I pray God your whole spirit and soul and body be
preserved blameless unto the coming of our
Lord Jesus Christ.
1 Thessalonians 5:23 (KJV)

Personal scriptures to meditate on:

- Matthew 10:28 – And fear not them which kill the body, but are not able to kill the soul: but rather fear him which is able to destroy both soul and body in hell.

- Isaiah 41:13 – For I the Lord thy God will hold thy right hand, saying unto thee, Fear not; I will help thee.

- John 10:10 – The thief cometh not, but for to steal, and to kill, and to destroy: I am come that they might have life, and that they might have it more abundantly.

- Acts 3:16 – Through faith in his name he has made me strong.

- Jeremiah 30:17 – For I will restore health unto thee, and I will heal thee of thy wounds, saith the Lord; because they called thee an Outcast, saying, This is Zion, whom no man seeketh after.

- Psalm 103:1 – Bless the Lord, O my soul: and all that is within me, bless his holy name.

- Jeremiah 33:6 – Behold, I will bring it health and cure, and I will cure them, and will reveal unto them the abundance of peace and truth.

- Matthew 11:28 – Come unto me, all ye that labour and are heavy laden, and I will give you rest.

- Matthew 11:29 – Take my yoke upon you, and learn of me; for I am meek and lowly in heart: and ye shall find rest unto your souls.

- Matthew 11:30 – For my yoke is easy, and my burden is light.

- Mark 5:34 – And he said unto her, Daughter, thy faith hath made thee whole; go in peace, and be whole of thy plague.

- Hebrews 11:1 – Now faith is the substance of things hoped for, the evidence of things not seen.

- Psalm 23:4 –Yea, though I walk through the valley of the shadow of death, I will fear no evil: for thou art with me; thy rod and thy staff they comfort me.

SECTION II

BETROTHAL

Chapter 5
The Man

After we have gotten those godly principles in place for matrimony, we are prepared for the betrothal, the engagement.

Engagement (or betrothal) is defined as the period of time between a marriage proposal and the marriage itself. In ancient biblical times, the man paid a dowry as a gift to the family of the woman he desired to marry. In most cases, the fathers arranged the match between the boy and the girl at a young age. Who pays the dowry differs across different cultures and religions.

In today's betrothals, the dowry usually comes in the form of a ring which is symbolic of a love union forever. A Hindu bride's family typically gives the groom a dowry. In Muslim cultures, the groom gives a gift or Mahr to his bride. A bride price is also commonly practiced by many major Black African cultures. The amount of the dowry depends on the particular culture. The dowry can be cash or come in the form of jewelry, furniture, property, a vehicle, or livestock.

In the story of Jacob and Rachel in the Bible, Jacob loved Rachel so much that he wanted to marry her, but did not have the money to pay a dowry to Laban her father (Genesis 29–31). So Jacob offered Laban seven years of free labor for Rachel's hand in marriage. But he got tricked and had to work another seven years before he could actual marry Rachel, because

Laban gave Jacob Leah, his oldest daughter, instead. If a man really loves a woman and really wants to marry that woman he will do whatever is necessary to marry the one he wants. It is the man who finds the wife.

Whoso findeth a wife findeth a good thing, and obtaineth favor of the Lord. Proverbs 18:22 (KJV)

Another biblical example, Abraham told one of his faithful and trusted servants to find his son Issac a wife. Abraham was getting up in age and had already lost his wife Sarah to death. Since Issac was the promised son, the nations would be blessed through Isaac after Abraham's death.

In Abraham instructions, the servant was not to get his son a wife from the Canaanites. Abraham did not want his son to be influenced by the Canaanite's wicked practices. So the servant was to return to Abraham's homeland and find his son a wife among his relatives. So upon the servant's arrival, he meets Rebekah at the well filling her pitchers with water and asked her for a drink.

Rebekah was a beautiful young virgin who happened to be Abraham brother's granddaughter. The servant found Rebekah to be kind and compassionate as she gave him and his camels water to drink. She was everything the servant had prayed to God for as a sign of the right person to be Issac's wife. While Rebekah was giving water to the camels, Abraham's servant gave Rebekah a golden earring (nose ring) and two bracelets for her hands weighing ten shekels (four ounces) for her kindness toward him and his camels.

Rebekah takes the servant and his men to her house. While the servant is at the house, he enters Rebekah into a marriage arrangement to be Issac's wife. Her father, Bethuel and her brother Laban make the arrangements. The servant gave Rebekah jewels of silver, and jewels of gold, and raiment when Bethuel and Laban agreed to let Rebekah go back with him. The servant also gave Rebekah's family gifts. In turn, the family gave Rebekah a maiden to take with her who was to care for her. Upon their arrival, Issac took Rebekah into his mother's tent and went into her and Rebekah became Issac's wife.

> *"And they blessed Rebekah and said unto her, Thou art our sister, be thou the mother of thousands of millions, and let they seed possess the gate of those which hate them."*
> *Genesis 24:60 (KJV)*

Going back to the beginning, in God's decision to create man, when God decided to create both male and female in His image (likeness), He asked for them to be fruitful, multiply, replenish the earth, and to have dominion over every living thing. At the same time, God instituted marriage and family as an important piece of creation.

During the dispensation of innocence, God planted a beautiful garden full of trees and a river that flowed into what is called the Garden of Eden. The river that flowed into the garden parted into four rivers that contained gold, bdellium, and onyx stone which flowed throughout the garden. However, God did not have anyone to till the land.

God caused a mist to come over the earth, and out of the dust of the ground God formed man and breathed into man's nostrils the breath of life (Pneuma) then man became a living soul. So man was put in the garden, the place of provision (the put place) to keep it and to dress it. Then God gave man instructions, from every tree in the garden man could eat freely, but God commanded man to not eat from the tree of the knowledge of good and evil. The result of disobeying the commandment to abstain was death.

God looking at everything He had made and said that it was good. Now, God realized every animal had a suitable mate but Adam. Then God decided that it was not good for man to be alone and caused a deep sleep to fall on Adam in order to make him a helper. As Adam slept, God took one of Adam's ribs and made woman. Then the marriage took place when God took her to Adam and Adam called his wife woman, saying bone of my bone and flesh of my flesh and that she shall be named Eve, the mother of all the living.

A very important pattern to follow and to note is before Adam married the woman, God put Adam in the garden, then gave Adam a job first, and then a wife. Adam was placed in the place of provision, given the job to maintain the garden, and a helper to help him meet the work/vision/instructions God had given him to carry out. Everything Adam and his wife needed was provided by God in the garden. We see how God had revealed Himself to be Jehovah-jireh, their provider.

> *Therefore shall a man leave his father and his mother, and shall cleave unto his wife: and they shall be one flesh. And they were both naked, the man and his wife, and were not ashamed.*
> *Genesis 2:24–25 (KJV)*

Look at what happens next: the serpent (Satan) shows up on the scene and approaches the woman, asking, "Hath God said, Ye shall not eat of every tree of the garden?" This detail is significant, as it raises the question of why the serpent spoke to Eve. It's important to note that once the man marries, Satan will visit the wife, who is the weaker vessel. Not that she is weak in physical strength but weaker emotionally, and she did not know what God had said exactly to the man because God did not give the instructions to the wife. Although the original command was given to Adam, Eve demonstrates her knowledge of it in their conversation. The serpent's approach may instead reflect a strategy to challenge and undermine the order established in the garden.

The text goes on to discuss the significance of Eve's role, noting that she possessed a womb and was therefore connected to the promise of offspring. A *womb* is defined as the organ in the lower body of a woman where offspring are conceived and in which they gestate before birth. Some interpret the serpent's actions as an attempt to corrupt or pervert the seed (offspring). Whenever Satan appears, it is with the intent to steal, kill, and destroy. Through cunning and craftiness, by appealing to the lust of the flesh, the lust of the eyes, and the pride of life, the serpent was able to deceive Eve into eating from the forbidden tree. After Eve partook of the fruit, she shared it with Adam, and he also ate. At that moment, their eyes were opened, and they became aware of their nakedness, sewing fig leaves together to make coverings.

When God came into the garden calling for Adam saying, "Adam where art thou?" Adam answered saying, "I heard thy voice in the garden, and I was afraid, because I was naked." God wanted to know who told Adam that he was naked because when God put Adam in the garden there was no knowledge revealed to Adam of his nakedness. The environment of the garden was of a pure and innocence state. So, God asked Adam if he had eaten from the tree of the knowledge of good and evil. Then Adam blamed Eve and said, "The woman whom thou gavest to be with me, she gave me of the tree and I did eat." It was that woman who made me disobey your commandment. It was all her fault. You know the one whom you gave to be with me? Yes her, it was her fault. Then God asked the woman to explain what she had done. Then Eve blamed the serpent saying that the serpent beguiled and tricked her into eating from the forbidden tree.

As a result of Adam's disobedience, they were banned from and kicked out of that beautiful garden (a.k.a. the fall of man to the dispensation of consciousness). The curse and judgment of God was released upon the serpent, the woman, and Adam. God said to the serpent first because he had deceived Eve, the serpent was cursed above the cattle, above every beast of the field; upon his belly he was to go, dust would the serpent eat all the days of his life, enmity would He put between the serpent and the woman and between the serpent's seed and the woman's seed.

Why did God say to the serpent enmity would be put between the serpent's seed and the woman's seed? Remember the woman has the womb. The serpent had deposited his seed of rebellion, disobedience, doubt, jealousy, pride, in other words, the seed of the kingdom of darkness into the woman.

And we can see the serpent's seed manifested in Eve's children between her first two sons, Cain and Abel. Cain got jealous of his brother Abel's first fruit offering to the Lord because God received Abel's offering but did not receive Cain's offering. Cain got angry and killed his brother because of it. Then God turned to the woman and said that He would increase sorrow in her conception and in the pain of childbearing, and her desire would be for her husband and he would rule over her. And God said to Adam, because he had listened to the voice of his wife and ate from the tree of the knowledge of good and evil which God had commanded him not to eat, cursed is the ground for thy sake and in sorrow Adam would eat from the ground by the sweat of his brow all the days of his life; whereas, before Adam was in the put place where all had been provided by God for him. The original design or state for man was to be in paradise, the put place where man had fellowship and communion with God with no interference or struggle with sin. Now, Adam was going to have to work by the sweat of his brow to eat from the ground that had been cursed with thorns and thistles.

God did not create man to be licentious. I believe today, men of the world, or men who are not following Godly principles to matrimony, have discovered that there is a shortage of good men "a famine in the land" if you will, and have determined that men do not have to put forth much effort to get a woman due to supply and demand. Men who do not follow Godly principles to matrimony have become promiscuous in their sexual matters to where they lack moral restraints and some do not even desire marriage anymore. Most men see themselves as a commodity who now have become men of privilege, who are self-centered, self-focused, and selfish. God created hu-

> *But, beloved, remember ye the words which were spoken before of the apostles of our Lord Jesus Christ; how that they told you there should be mockers in the last time, who should walk after their own ungodly lusts. These be they who separate themselves, sensual, having not the Spirit.*
> *Jude 17–19 (KJV)*

manity to love and to worship Him. We love God because He first loved us. If men would allow the love of God to grow in him, a man's will and affections would change so that God's love would replace man's mindset of being self-centered, privileged, and selfish.

As part of my personal journey, I had married a man who had the mindset that I should have been glad to have been married to him because there were so many other women who wished they could have been in my place. Therefore, I should not be questioning his faithfulness to the marriage. It really is a shame that licentious men see women as subservient to man and as a means to an end. I am thankful that I loved myself enough to know that I deserved to be loved too.

> Husbands, love your wives, even as Christ also loved the church, and gave himself for it; that he might sanctify and cleanse it with the washing of water by the word, that he might present it to himself a glorious church, not having spot, or wrinkle, or any such thing; but that it should be holy and without blemish. So ought men to love their wives as their own bodies. He that loveth his wife loveth himself.
>
> Ephesians 5:25–28 (KJV)

Personal scriptures to meditate on:

- Psalm 1:1 – Blessed is the man that walketh not in the counsel of the ungodly, nor standeth in the way of sinners, nor sitteth in the seat of the scornful.

- Proverb 16:9 – A man's heart deviseth his way: but the Lord directeth his steps.

- 1 Corinthians 13:11 – When I was a child, I spake as a child, I understood as a child, I thought as a child: but when I became a man, I put away childish things.

- Romans 13:13-14 – Let us walk honestly, as in the day; not in rioting and drunkenness, not in chambering and wantonness, not in strife and envying. But put ye on the Lord Jesus Christ, and make not provision for the flesh, to fulfil the lusts thereof.

- Genesis 1:26-27 – And God said, Let us make man in our image, after our likeness: and let them have dominion over the fish of the sea, and over the fowl of the air, and over the cattle, and over all the earth, and over every creeping thing that creepeth upon the earth. So God created man in his own image, in the image of God created he him; male and female created he them.

- Psalm 32:8 – I will instruct thee and teach thee in the way which thou shalt go: I will guide thee with mine eye.

- Micah 6:8 – He hath shewed thee, O man, what is good; and what doth the Lord require of thee, but to do justly, and to love mercy, and to walk humbly with thy God?

- 2 Timothy 2:15 – Study to shew thyself approved unto God, a workman that needeth not to be ashamed, rightly dividing the word of truth.

- Ephesians 4:13 – Till we all come in the unity of the faith, and of the knowledge of the Son of God, unto a perfect man, unto the measure of the stature of the fulness of Christ.

• Ephesians 4:14 – That we henceforth be no more children, tossed to and fro, and carried about with every wind of doctrine, by the sleight of men, and cunning craftiness, whereby they lie in wait to deceive.

• Ecclesiastes 10:2 – A wise man's heart is at his right hand; but a fool's heart at his left.

• Ecclesiastes 2:26a – For God giveth to a man that is good in his sight wisdom, and knowledge, and joy.

Chapter 6
The Woman

In the Garden of Eden, Eve became the first woman and became the mother of all living things. Because of Eve's disobedience, women today suffer the pain of child bearing and have a desire to be loved and respected by their husbands, but the man only wants to rule over her.

There seems to be a disconnect between the woman and the man today because the man see's the woman as being subservient to him and as someone to just rule over. The woman is not seen as a valuable asset to the man unless he can pervert her. Therefore, the woman is left with a void in her heart that she tries to fill, but really only God can fill that void.

In the biblical days, the woman got married to a man she did not know, but because of the beliefs in her culture, religion, and traditions, the woman married accordingly. During those biblical days, the women eagerly took on the responsibility of marriage. For the most part, a modern woman today has to be in love with the man before she will marry him.

It is time for women to come to know their worth and value. Women, we are fearfully and wonderfully made, we must know that before we can expect a man to love us. We have to learn how to love and appreciate who God has made us to be. In other words, we must love and respect ourselves first.

We are looking for love in all the wrong places. Love is not a romantic feeling. Love is God because God is Love. When a woman starts out a relationship with God as her first love, I believe a woman can then build her marriage upon that rock, which is a firm foundation instead of upon sand which shifts.

When marriage is built upon a rock, the storms of life may blow, but the marriage has a better chance of withstanding what comes against it. At that point, the marriage has become like a fortified city. Now, being a woman, wife, and mother is not an easy job. That is why the wisdom of God is needed to give us the know-how to become a woman of God, a godly wife, and a godly mother. Through the holy spirit wisdom will be revealed to us. All we have to do is ask God for wisdom. He gives wisdom liberally to those who ask.

I believe the woman has to be mature in her relationship with Christ first in order to apply godly principles to any situation. I know for me, when I got married, I did not even know who I was, not to mention how to be a wife and mother. It was just by the grace of God that my children were not damaged beyond repair. I am so thankful that my children are loving, intelligent, responsible, independent, hardworking, and self-sufficient adults, to which I owe a lot of thanks to their father, who loves them dearly and has always been there for his children.

In the Bible there was a woman named Naomi in the story of Naomi and Ruth, her daughter-in-law. Naomi was a wife and mother who was wise and full of faith and became a source of strength for her family.

Naomi's husband Elimelech took her, their two sons, and

their wives to Moab to escape the famine in Judah in search for food. Naomi followed her husband away from the land the Lord had promised to bless and ended up losing her husband and all of her sons in Moab. She found herself empty and without male protection in a strange land with her two daughter-in-laws, which was God's judgment upon her.

Bethlehem in the Hebrew means House of Bread, a place where God's provision is provided. However, God used Namoi's situation to take her back to her home in Bethlehem (House of Bread) to replace her emptiness with a fullness that only God could provide.

When we leave God's provision and protection we open ourselves up to God's judgment. But God does not use His judgment to destroy us; He uses His judgment to get us back on track with Him. One of the daughter-in-laws, Ruth went with Naomi back to Bethlehem, and Ruth ended up marrying Boaz a distant relative of Elimelech, her late father-in-law.

So through Boaz, Naomi and Ruth were redeemed by a kinsman-redeemer. The kinsman-redeemer is a male relative who, according to various laws of the Pentateuch, had the responsibility to act on behalf of a relative who is in trouble, danger, or need. I am reminded of another redeemer, Jesus Christ, who rescued us from the penalty of sin.

I am reminded of another women of the Bible who was full of wisdom, an orphan and a Jew by the name of Hadassah (Esther) who was the most unlikely person to become a queen of a great empire of King Xerxes (Ahasuerus). God chooses the foolish things of the world to confound the wise.

Through Queen Esther's heroic act she was able to redeem

her nation from the plot of Haman. The king had just promoted Haman to a high ranking position as adviser; therefore, all of the king's servants were to bow and reverence Haman as he passed through the gates.

Queen Esther's uncle Mordecai also stood at the gate every day to keep up to date on how Queen Esther was doing. Some men asked Mordecai why he did not bow and give reverence to Haman as the king had commanded for the king's servants to do. Mordecai responded because he was a Jew. The word got back to Haman that Mordecai refused to bow when he came through the gate because he was a Jew.

Haman was furious. After Haman found out that Mordecai was a Jew, he devised a plot to annihilate all the Jews. Haman went to the king and told him that there were some people scattered throughout the kingdom who had different laws, and they were not keeping the king's law. Haman asked the King to let it be written that those people be destroyed.

Queen Esther found out about Haman's plan to destroy all the Jews. Well, that did not exempt Queen Esther, because she was a Jew as well. However, being favored by the king, Queen Esther devised a plan against Haman's plot to reveal to the king what Haman had planned and the reason why Haman plotted to kill the Jews.

Queen Esther risked her own life to go before the king, because she was not supposed to go before the king unless the king had called for her. Haman's plot was reversed on him and Haman was the one who was killed, and the Jews were saved.

See, a woman may have to carry a lot of responsibility on her shoulders not just for herself, but for her marriage, children, and ministry. A woman cannot be a foolish woman.

Remember that the woman was made to be a wife and not a concubine. Under the law, the kings had concubines. A *concubine* is defined as a woman who cohabits with a man to whom she is not legally married, especially one regarded as socially or sexually subservient; mistress. That is why as women we have to value ourselves enough and do the inner work because in the end we will be better for it.

It has been my experience nowadays men do not have to put forth much effort when it comes to the opposite sex. The men will start off with conversations to win the women's trust. Then, it is like they are waiting on the woman to fall and or make the first move from the casual conversations to sex, especially if she is needy and or desperate. I believe today's vernacular is 'thirsty'.

When we learn better, we do better. If a man is serious about the woman, he will tell her. The woman will not have to guess about the relationship. One thing to note is that most of the kings in the Bible were wicked; therefore, it is imperative that we follow after the principles of the Kingdom of Heaven and not man, which will ultimate lead to peace of mind, because He is the Prince of Peace.

The Bible holds women in high esteem. It teaches that women are co-bearers of the image of God, and that He crowned women with honor and glory, and gave women charge to exercise dominion over the earth. Remember God gave them both dominion over the earth, fish of sea, and the fowls of the air.

There are two women in the Bible who had an enormous respect for God's Word: Eunice and Lois, Timothy's mother and grandmother. They made sure Timothy was taught the scriptures and doctrine.

Modern day women often do not esteem the Word of God and are unwilling to exert the effort to sharpen their personal Bible study habits and are not even concerned about applying the word of God to their lives.

We must become like the Samaritan woman Jesus met at the well who had five husbands and the one she was with was not hers. After spending time in Jesus' presence and communing with Him, she perceived Jesus to be a prophet. She was excited and ran and told the people in the cities to come see a man "who told me all about myself." She was operating in the gift of an Evangelist.

Women have a responsibility to develop their ability and their understanding of the scripture correctly; if not, women are more likely to fall susceptible to error by every wind of doctrine. We do not want to be like that silly woman who was forever learning but never coming into the knowledge of God for herself. Women must become students of the Word of God to be able to help guide their families in the ways of the Lord.

Study to shew thyself approved unto God,
a workman that needeth not be ashamed,
rightly dividing the word of truth.
2 Timothy 2:15 (KJV)

Personal scriptures to meditate on:

- Proverb 4:7 – Wisdom is the principal thing; therefore get wisdom: and with all thy getting understanding.

- Psalm 37:4 – Delight thyself also in the Lord: and he shall give thee the desires of thine heart.

- 1 Corinthians 7:34 – The unmarried woman careth for the things of the Lord, that she may be holy both in body and in spirit.

- Proverbs 31:30 – Charm is deceitful, and beauty is vain: but a woman that feareth the Lord, she shall be praised.

- Romans 12:1 – I beseech you therefore, brethren, by the mercies of God, that ye present your bodies a living sacrifice, holy, acceptable unto God, which is your reasonable service.

- Proverbs 11:2 – When pride cometh, then cometh shame: but with the lowly is wisdom.

- 2 Corinthians 6:14 – Be ye not unequally yoked together with unbelievers: for what fellowship hath righteousness with unrighteousness? and what communion hath light with darkness?

- Proverbs 4:23 – Keep thy heart with all diligence; for out of it are the issues of life.

- Psalm 119:10 – With my whole heart have I sought thee: O let me not wander from thy commandments.

- Ecclesiastes 3:1 – To every thing there is a season, and a time to every purpose under the heaven.

- Proverbs 14:1 – Every wise woman buildeth her house: but the foolish plucketh it down with her hands.

- Proverbs 1:7 – The fear of the Lord is the beginning of knowledge: but fools despise wisdom and instruction.

- James 1:5 – If any of you lack wisdom, let him ask of God, that giveth to all men liberally, and upbraideth not; and it shall be given him.

- Proverbs 2:6 – For the Lord giveth wisdom: out of his mouth cometh knowledge and understanding.

- Proverbs 16:16a – How much better is it to get wisdom than gold.

- 1 Corinthians 7:8 – I say therefore to the unmarried and widows, it is good for them if they abide as I. (single)

- 1 Corinthians 7:9 – But if they cannot contain, let them marry: for it is better to marry than to burn.

- Proverbs 31:10 – Who can find a virtuous woman? For her price is far above rubies.

- Song of Solomon 2:7 – Do not stir up, nor awake love, before its time.

SECTION III
COVENANT

Chapter 7
Covenant

In this section, we are going to look at the covenant relationship and how the Holy Spirit played a role in creation in the beginning. To me, a covenant is a promise or an agreement made between two people. As a noun, *covenant* is an agreement, usually formal, between two or more persons to do or not do something specified. As a verb, *covenant* is defined as to enter into a covenant or to promise by a covenant. The covenant will only be in effect as long as the specified conditions continue to be met.

In the Bible, several covenants were made, including a marriage covenant, which was made between two people. As we can recall, Adam and Eve made the first marriage covenant in the Bible, and they were to be fruitful, multiply, and replenish the earth. The marriage covenant was made between one man and one woman coming together as one flesh, which was God's original plan for marriage.

To "become one flesh" is about having oneness, harmony, and agreement, which makes up a unified front. When I think of unity, I am reminded of the day of Pentecost when they were all in one accord, and they all spoke in tongues as the Spirit gave them utterance, which was a promise fulfilled that God would send the Holy Spirit.

Oneness is being of a like-mind, having the same Agape love one for another, being in one accord and letting nothing that is done be done for a selfish reason. Do everything for one another in lowliness of mind and to esteem the other above oneself.

Everything in the Kingdom of God operates by faith. Without faith it is impossible to please God. Faith is the substance of the things you are hoping for and the evidence of the things that are not seen yet.

> Till we all come in the unity of the faith, and of the knowledge of the Son of God, unto a perfect man, unto the measure of the stature of the fullness of Christ: That we henceforth be no more children, tossed to and fro, and carried about with every wind of doctrine, by the sleight of men, and cunning craftiness, whereby they lie in wait to deceive; But speaking the truth in love, may grow up into him in all things, which is the head, even Christ: From whom the whole body fitly joined together and compacted by that which every joint supplieth, according to the effectual working in the measure of every part, maketh increase of the body unto the edifying of itself in love.
> Ephesians 4:13–16 (KJV)

In ancient biblical times, marriages were negotiated between families and often involved an agreement on specific conditions and the payment of a bride price or dowry, depending on the culture. Fathers were more concerned about the marriages of their sons than their daughters, because there was not an expense in marrying off the daughters. Instead, the father of the groom had to give a bride price to the future father-in-law when marrying off his son.

The Abrahamic Covenant contained all that God began to do, has since done throughout history, and will continue to do. In other words, all of God's plans for humanity grew out of this covenant. The Abrahamic covenant has three parts: national, personal, and universal. God told Abram, "I will make you a great nation" (national); "I will bless you and make your name great and you shall be a blessing" (personal); "In you all families of the earth shall be blessed" (universal) (Genesis 12:1–3, KJV).

> *That whosoever believeth in him should not perish, but have eternal life. For God so loved the world, that he gave his only begotten Son, that whosoever believeth in him should not perish, but have everlasting life.*
>
> *John 3:15–16 (KJV)*

God renewed His covenant with Abram on several occasions, one being when God said, "Unto thy seed have I given this land, from the river of Egypt unto the great river, the river Euphrates" (Genesis 15:18–21, KJV). God renews His covenant with Abram, but this time God changes Abram's name to Abraham, meaning 'father of many nations' signaling that he would be fruitful and that kings would come from his nation.

God said, "I will establish my covenant between me and thee and thy seed after thee in their generations for an everlasting covenant, to be a God unto thee, and to thy seed after thee" (Genesis 17:7, KJV). For the law was given by Moses, but grace and truth came by Jesus Christ. In the Covenant God made with Abraham, grace was introduced by God when He said, and "to thy seed after thee in their generations for an everlasting covenant."

The Mosaic Covenant (Law of Moses), also known as the Old Covenant, is a conditional covenant that was made between God and the Israelites at Mount Sinai. The Mosaic Covenant and its laws were given to the people at Mount Sinai when Moses went up to the mountain a voice called unto him out of the mountain saying:

> Thus shalt thou say to the house of Jacob, and tell the children of Israel; Ye have seen what I did unto the Egyptians, and how I bare you on eagles' wings, and brought you unto myself. Now therefore, if ye will obey my voice indeed, and keep my covenant, then ye shall be a peculiar treasure unto me above all people; for all the earth is mine: And ye shall be unto me a kingdom of priests, and an holy nation.
> And all the people answered together, and said, All that the Lord hath spoken we will do.
> Exodus 19:3–6, 8 (KJV)

What is ironic about the Mosaic covenant is that it was not about developing a personal relationship with God but about communicating what the Israelites should do as a people who had been delivered from Egypt and had been brought to God as His people. The Israelites were to obey the law.

In my study of the children of Israel, they really had a problem with obeying God's commandments. The children of Israel violated the covenant agreement of being faithful. They rejected the knowledge of God and His law. They had become proud and stiff-necked. They were engaging in idolatry and cult prostitution. They were trusting everybody except the one who had shown His love for them and called them His own people. Throughout the Bible, I have found God to remain faithful to the children of Israel by not utterly destroying them, even though they willfully disobeyed His commandments. God would always send a prophet to tell the people of their wrongful doing and compel them to repent.

In the Book of Hosea, God used Hosea's marriage as an example to show how the Israelites were treating their God. Hosea was married to an unfaithful woman named Gomer. This was meant to get the people to stop their promiscuity, idolatry, and iniquity and for them to return to God in humility and faithfulness, and if they would not return, chastisement would follow in the form of judgment. But after judgment, Israel would be restored.

In their restoration, Israel would call Him Ishi (My Husband) and not Baali (My Master) because He will take the names of Baalim out of Israel mouth and that He would make a covenant with Israel and they would be betrothed unto Him forever, and that they would know the Lord.

> Therefore, behold, I will allure her, and bring her into the wilderness, and speak comfortably unto her. And I will give her her vineyards from thence, and the valley of Achor for a door of hope: and she shall sing there, as in the days of her youth, and as in the day when she came up out of the land of Egypt. And it shall be at that day, saith the Lord, that thou shalt call me Ishi; and shalt call me no more Baali. For I will take away the names of Baalim out of her mouth, and they shall no more be remembered by their name. And in that day will I make

a covenant for them with the beasts of the field and
with the fowls of heaven, and with the creeping things
of the ground: and I will break the bow and the sword
and the battle out of the earth, and will make them to
lie down safely. And I will betroth thee unto me for ever;
yea, I will betroth thee unto me in righteousness, and in
judgment, and in lovingkindness, and in mercies. I will
even betroth thee unto me in faithfulness:
and thou shalt know the Lord.
Hosea 2:14–20 (KJV)

So, if the Israelites wanted to be blessed they would obey the law, and if they would not obey the law they would be punished. The Israelites found themselves always struggling to keep the commandments of the law, which resulted in some not entering into the Promised Land.

God had separated Israel to be a called-out nation who worshiped the covenant-keeping God. The Mosaic Law is known to be a schoolmaster that revealed to the people their sins and their need for a Savior.

The schoolmaster was what the children of Israel needed because they had been slaves for several hundred years in Egypt learning about paganism, idol worship, and idol gods. Now the New Covenant is confirmed in Christ. During the Lords Supper Jesus Christ said, "This cup is the new testament in my blood which is shed for you" (Luke 22:20). When Christ came He did not come to abolish the law but to fulfill the law.

The scripture hath concluded all under sin, that the
promise by faith of Jesus Christ might be given to them

that believe. But before faith came, we were kept under
the law, shut up unto the faith which should afterwards
be revealed. Wherefore the law was our schoolmaster to
bring us unto Christ, that we might be justified by faith.
But after that faith is come, we are
no longer under a schoolmaster.
Galatians 3:22–25 (KJV)

Under the Old Covenant, God was married to the children of Israel. He was their husband who was trying to get Israel to return to Him. Now, under the New Covenant, Jesus Christ is the bridegroom and head over the church, who is His bride.

The marriage covenant relationship is symbolic of Christ's relationship to the church. The enemy is deceiving some husbands into believing that they can abdicate their responsibility to the wife and still maintain the title of headship. This is a demonic spirit, called the Ahab spirit, which is trying to work through the husband. This allows another demonic spirit called Jezebel to operate through the wife to take on the responsibility of the head without the title of headship.

In my experience with the Jezebel spirit working through the wife, she does not need the title of headship because as long as she is functioning on behalf of the head she would still be in control and running things.

After creation, God became upset with man and how wicked man had become. First it was Adam and Eve who ate from the tree of knowledge of good and evil, then to Cain murdering his brother Abel, to one of Cain's descendants Lamech, who had two wives, which was against God's law, and then the preoccupation with evil in man's heart. God regretted creating man and decided to destroy man from the face of the earth.

In God's decision to destroy all flesh due to man's wickedness, God made a covenant with Noah to build an ark so when He sent the flood upon the earth to destroy it, Noah, his family, and every animal Noah put in the ark would be saved. God sent a rainbow as a reminder of the covenant He made with Noah not to destroy every living creature of all flesh again with a flood.

Personal scriptures to meditate on:

- Hebrews 9:15 – And for this cause he is the mediator of the new testament, that by means of death for the redemption of the transgressions that were under the first testament, they which are called might receive the promise of eternal inheritance.

- Isaiah 61:10 – I will greatly rejoice in the Lord, my soul shall be joyful in my God; for he hath clothed me with the garments of salvation, he hath covered me with the robe of righteousness, as a bridegroom decketh himself with ornaments, and as a bride adorneth herself with her jewels.

- Isaiah 54:5 – For thy Maker is thine husband; the Lord of hosts is his name; and thy Redeemer the Holy One of Israel; The God of the whole earth shall he be called.

- Matthew 19:6 – Wherefore they are no more twain, but one flesh. What therefore God hath joined together; let not man put asunder.

- Genesis 1:27 – So God created man in his own image, in the image of God created he him; male and female created he them.

- Malachi 2:14 – Yet ye say, Wherefore? Because the Lord hath been witness between thee and the wife of thy youth, against whom thou hast dealt treacherously: yet is she thy companion, and the wife of thy covenant.

- Song of Solomon 8:6 – Set me as a seal upon thine heart, as a seal upon thine arm: for love is strong as death; jealousy is cruel as the grave: the coals thereof are coals of fire, which hath a most vehement flame.

- Ephesians 4:2–3 – With all lowliness and meekness, with longsuffering, forbearing one another in love; endeavouring to keep the unity of the Spirit in the bond of peace.

- Ecclesiastes 4:9 – Two are better than one; because they have a good reward for their labour.

- Genesis 2:24 – Therefore shall a man leave his father and his mother, and shall cleave unto his wife: and they shall be one flesh.

- Mark 10:9 – What therefore God hath joined together, let not man put asunder.

- Romans 13:8 – Owe no man any thing, but to love one another: for he that loveth another hath fulfilled the law.

- 1 Corinthians 16:14 – Let all your things be done with charity.

- Psalm 143:8 – Cause me to hear thy lovingkindness in the morning; for in thee do I trust: cause me to know the way wherein I should walk; for I lift up my soul unto thee.

- 1 John 4:16 – And we have known and believed the love that God hath to us. God is love; and he that dwelleth in love dwelleth in God, and God in him.

- John 15:12 – This is my commandment, That ye love one another, as I have loved you.

Chapter 8
Role of the Husband

In this section, we will look at the parallel in Ephesians 5 of the role of Christ over the church and the role of the husband as a type of Christ in the marriage-covenant relationship. First, Christ is the head of the body, the church, and He is the beginning and the firstborn from the dead. As a matter of fact, Christ is the head of every man, and man is the head of the wife, and God is the head of Christ. Therefore, the husband is the head of his body, the woman who is bone of his bones and flesh of his flesh, because the woman came out of the rib of man. The woman completes the man.

The scripture tells us that the woman is the glory of the man. And that the woman is of the man and that the woman was created for the man. And for that very reason the woman ought to have power on her head because of the angels. In other words, the woman needs a husband to cover her. Nevertheless, "neither is the man without the woman, neither the woman without the man, in the Lord. For as the woman is of the man, even so is the man also by the woman; but all things are of God" (1 Corinthians 11:11–12, KJV).

Christ is the firstborn from the dead, which would mean that first, the husband needs to be dead to the old man and resurrected as a new creation in Christ.

Under the New Covenant, Christ is the head of the church and is the savior of the body. Therefore, one of the roles of the husband would be a position of self-sacrifice in the marriage covenant. Just as Christ demonstrated His love for the church, by dying for it so He could sanctify or cleanse the church by the washing of water by the word, that He might present the church back to Himself as a glorious church, not having spot or wrinkle but that the church should be holy and without blemish. I believe this is one of the reasons that divorce is so high among Christians because husbands are not in proper alignment with Christ, with a proper understanding of how to be in the position of headship without being contentious, dogmatic, and domineering.

> *If so be that ye have heard him, and have been taught by him, as the truth is in Jesus: That ye put off concerning the former conversation the old man, which is corrupt according to the deceitful lusts; And be renewed in the spirit of your mind; And that ye put on the new man, which after God is created in righteousness and true holiness.*
> *Ephesians 4:21–24 (KJV)*

Christ functions as the spiritual leader over the church, whom the husband should align himself with as being the spiritual leader over his bride. By the husband becoming a servant leader, that would mean that he leads by example so his bride can follow him. Some husbands see being the head over his wife to mean he has the right to boss her around, not so!

Even though, Christ was equal to God, He submitted His will unto God and humbled Himself unto death. In the marriage covenant, the husband and the wife are to submit to one another in the fear and admiration of the Lord.

In order for the husband to become the spiritual leader

over his wife, he has to leave his father and mother's house and cleave to his wife in order to take on the responsibility of spiritual leadership for his own family unit. The order of the marriage covenant dynamic is first Christ then the husband, then the wife and then the children.

> For the husband is the head of the wife, even as Christ
> is the head of the church: and he is the saviour of the
> body. Therefore as the church is subject unto Christ, so
> let the wives be unto their own husbands in everything.
> Husbands, love your wives, even as Christ also loved the
> church, and gave himself for it; That He might sanctify
> and cleanse it with the washing of water by the word,
> That He might present it to himself a glorious church,
> not having spot, or wrinkle, or any such thing; but that it
> should be holy and without blemish. So ought
> men to love their wives as their own bodies.
> He that loveth his wife loveth himself.
> Ephesians 5:23–28 (KJV)

The role of the husband is not to domesticate or to tame his wife as if she is a wild animal. Wild animals need to be trained, not a human being who has a free will. When an animal is domesticated, the genetics of that particular breed is permanently modified to a predisposition toward humans. That is the mindset of the old man and it must die and the mind renewed.

According to scripture, unless the corn of wheat fall into the ground and die, it abides alone. Also, the husband is not to tame his wife as if she is a dog. The word *tame* is defined as an animal who is not dangerous or frightened of people; as of a person, willing to cooperate; not controversial; to make less powerful and easier to control. There in the definition lies the problem. Who told you that a woman needed to be tamed? Dogs are trained how to obey through obedience training, not adults. Wives are to be loved as Christ loved the church and gave Himself for it. This is where the scripture is used out of context as a means to an end, the wife is to obey and submit to her husband; whereas, the scripture tells both the husband and the wife to submit one to another.

If this old mindset is not corrected or changed, the only person enjoying the marriage will be the husband, because the wife will be in bondage and unfulfilled. The woman was created in God's image and likeness, just like the man; God created them, not just him.

In the garden before God manifested Eve, Adam had named all the animals then God said to Adam that it was not good for man to be alone and that He was going to make Adam a suitable helper. If the woman was to be treated like an animal, then Adam could have just married one of those animals. Instead, God caused a sleep to come over Adam and took out of Adams' side rib and made woman. When Adam saw her, he named her woman because she was bone of his bone and flesh of his flesh.

If the husband is going to function in the role as Christ functions in the role toward the church, any type of control, manipulation, and dominance will not work in the marriage covenant. I don't care how good the man may look, how much money the man may make, whether he is an alpha male or not. Society has bewitched us! As a matter of fact, control, manipulation, and domination are fruits that come straight from the kingdom of darkness.

Be ye not unequally yoked together with unbelievers:
for what fellowship hath righteousness with unrighteousness? And what communion hath light with
darkness? And what concord hath Christ with Belial? or
what part hath he that believeth with an infidel? And
what agreement hath the temple of God with idols? for
ye are the temple of the living God; as God hath said, I
will dwell in them, and walk in them; and I will be their
God, and they shall be my people. Wherefore come out
from among them, and be ye separate, saith the Lord
and touch not the unclean thing; and I will receive you.
And will be a Father unto you, and ye shall be my sons
and daughters, saith the Lord Almighty.
2 Corinthians 6:14–18 (KJV)

For the longest time, the church has only dealt with being unequally yoked with unbelievers. In other words, if you are a
believer, do not enter into a marriage covenant with an un-
believer. However, the revelation goes deeper because the
problem the church is facing concerns believers who are in a
marriage covenant but are struggling within their covenant
relationship to stay together.

We must remember the soul was not saved when we accepted Christ as our Savior. Until we renew our minds, we still
have the same mindset as before we accepted Christ, which
is the opposite mindset of "let this mind be in you which was
also in Christ Jesus" (Philippians 2:5). In letting this mind be
in you we are allowing Christ to also be our Lord! Our obedience is directed to God. Working out our own soul salvation

is to apply salvation with fear and trembling. In other words to have proper respect in our dealings with one another. Our true obedience comes from a place of reverence and not fear.

Wherefore, my beloved, as ye have always obeyed, not as in my presence only, but now much more in my absence, work out your own salvation with fear and trembling. For it is God which worketh in you both to will and to do of His good pleasure. Philippians 2:12–13 (KJV)

I can testify of this in my own life, I was married to a narcissist, but at the time I was not aware. A narcissist is a person who is overly self-involved and often vain and selfish. From a psychoanalysis view, a narcissist is a person who experiences or exhibits narcissism, deriving erotic gratification from admiration of their own physical or mental attributes. If you would allow me to put the definition in layman's terms, it means being a person who is full of himself or herself.

In the beginning of my relationship with my husband, I did not allow myself time to get to know the man I was about to marry. I based my decision to marry on surface information those things which I could see. I focused on all the externals while the internals were hidden from me.

In the beginning, the marriage was wonderful. We spent a lot of time together and I was happy and laughing again. We spent so much time together I began to feel smothered, which felt like life was being squeezed out of me by a python snake who would kill his prey. I found myself in a situation where I did not have meaningful time to myself to do the essentials of life like work, run household errands, time with my family, time shopping alone without being called 1,000 times a day. Sometimes I would not answer the phone on purpose, but then the calls would be repeated back-to-back like someone was in a panic or crisis, so I would breakdown and answer the phone. Whenever I answered the phone, I would be asked in a rude tone of voice questions like, "What you doing?" and "Where you at?"

At first, the attention was flattering, but that attention became obsessive, oppressive, and depressive. I fell into a state of depression where I had to seek mental health care in which I was prescribed an antidepressant to take just for me to maintain sanity. I went from a person who had excellent health to good health. I started having high blood pressure issues, became pre-diabetic, had gastrointestinal issues, and even some female issues.

I tried to make the marriage work. I had done every thing I knew to do after 11 years of trying, but nothing was ever good enough. It was always too long or too short. If my husband gave me a compliment, he would cancel it out by saying something negative, trying to tear me down and break my spirit. He rarely said thank you. He had a sense of entitlement. When I finally came to my senses and realized that the devil was working through my husband trying to bring my soul under captivity, I stopped trying to please my husband, even though we were both believers.

There was a demonic spirit at work through my husband trying to muzzle me and keep me from teaching the Word of God. Whenever the devil shows up on any scene he comes only to steal, kill, and destroy. The devil is not trying to celebrate us.

Jesus Christ died so that we might have eternal life. He paid the price for our sins by shedding His blood on the cross so that we might have life and have life more abundantly. We are to be full of joy and to walk in the light. Christ is our advocate sitting at the right hand of the Father. We are to love God with all of our heart, soul, mind, and strength so that when we are tempted by the lust of the flesh, lust of the eyes, and the pride of life, we will be able to resist the enemy. We are to beware of the anti-christ spirit and let no man deceive us with smooth words and flattery of speech. The scripture tells us if we abide in Christ and He will abide in us so we can bear fruit.

> Behold, what manner of love the Father hath bestowed upon us, that we should be called the sons of God: therefore the world knoweth us not, because it knew him not. Beloved, now are we the sons of God, and it doth not yet appear what we shall be: but we know that, when he shall appear, we shall be like him; for we shall see him as he is. And every man that hath this hope in him purifieth himself, even as he is pure. Whosoever committeth sin transgresseth also the law: for sin is the transgression of the law. And ye know that he was manifested to take away our sins; and in him is no sin. Whosover abideth in him sinneth not: whosoever sinneth hath not seen him, neither known him. Little children, let no man deceive you: he that doeth righteousness is righteous, even as He is righteous. He that committeth sin is of the devil; for the devil sinneth from the beginning. For this purpose the Son of God was manifested, the he might destroy the works of the devil.
>
> 1 John 3:1–8 (KJV)

Personal scriptures to meditate on:

- Proverbs 18:22 – Whoso findeth a wife findeth a good thing, and obtaineth favor of the Lord.

- Genesis 2:18 – And the Lord God said, it is not good that the man should be alone; I will make him an help meet for him.

- Genesis 2:24 – Therefore shall a man leave his father and his mother, and shall cleave unto his wife: and they shall be one flesh.

- Ephesians 5:28 – So ought men to love their wives as their own bodies. He that loveth his wife loveth himself.

- 1 Corinthians 13:4–5 – Love suffereth long, and is kind; love envieth not; love vaunteth not itself, is not puffed up. Doth not behave itself unseemly, seeketh not her own, is not easily provoked, thinketh no evil."

- 1 Corinthians 13:6 – Love rejoiceth not in iniquity, but rejoiceth in the truth.

- 1 Corinthians 13:7 – Love beareth all things, believeth all things, hopeth all things, endureth all things.

- 1 Corinthians 13:8 – Love never faileth, but whether there be prophecies, they shall fail; whether there be tongues, they shall cease; whether there be knowledge, it shall vanish away.

- 1 Peter 3:7 – Likewise, ye husbands, dwell with your wives according to knowledge, giving honour unto the wife, as unto the weaker vessel, and as being heirs together of the grace of life; that your prayers be not hindered.

- Colossians 3:19 – Husbands, love your wives, and be not bitter against them.

- John 12:24 – Except a corn of wheat fall into the ground and die, it abideth alone: but if it die, it bringeth forth much fruit.

• Colossians 2:6 – As ye have therefore received Christ Jesus the Lord, so walk ye in him

• Colossians 2:7 – Rooted and built up in Him, and stablished in the faith, as ye have been taught, abounding therein with thanksgiving.

• Colossians 2:8 – Beware lest any man spoil you through philosophy and vain deceit, after the tradition of men, after the rudiments of the world, and not after Christ."

• Colossians 2:11 – In whom also ye are circumcised with the circumcision made without hands, in putting off the body of the sins of the flesh by the circumcision of Christ.

• Colossians 2:12 – Buried with him in baptism, wherein also ye are risen with him through the faith of the operation of God, who hath raised him from the dead.

Chapter 9
Role of the Wife

In this section we are going to look at the role of the wife in contrast to Ephesians 5. In looking at the wife's role from a symbolic standpoint as a type of the church, the bride. Apostle Paul explains that the church exists and functions only by reason of its essential relationship to its head, Christ Jesus, who has been resurrected and exalted, is without needs, but is not independent of anything. As the head, Christ is incomplete without the body, which is the church. Therefore, the body and the head are one in the truest sense.

The church, the bride, is to submit to Christ. Therefore, the wife is to submit to her husband as unto the Lord. Now, submission is where we lose a lot of women due to bad experiences, or they know someone who has had a bad experience with submission. We often hear the woman is to submit unto her husband, and we miss the part about as unto the Lord.

If a woman's submission is coerced, demanded by force or use of intimidation or in any way other than voluntarily, the woman does not have to submit. Submission does not mean the woman is unequal or less than in the marriage covenant relationship. Since both the husband and the wife are equally submitting one to another, you cannot have two heads. Therefore, the wife voluntarily comes under the submission of her husband by subjecting herself to his leadership. Christ is the perfect example of this. Christ was equal to God, but He put on the form of a servant and became obedient unto death. Christ is a servant and not a dictator. Christ's desire is for us to submit to Him, but He will not force us to. We never lose our will to not submit to Christ.

> Let this mind be in you, which was also in Christ Jesus: Who, being in the form of God, thought it not robbery to be equal with God: But made Himself of no reputation, and took upon him the form of a servant, and was made in the likeness of men: And being found in fashion as a man, he humbled himself, and became obedient unto death, even the death of the cross.
> Philippians 2:5–8 (KJV)

First, the wife will need to have her own personal relationship with Christ prior to becoming a wife. We learn submission by submitting to the Lord. *Submission* has become a bad word to some ladies, and I get it, I do; however, in God's original plan for marriage, God never intended for a woman to be over a man in a marriage-covenant relationship.

Please do not misunderstand what I am saying. This does not have anything to do with ministering, preaching, teaching the word of God. If we go back to the garden, remember who the serpent approached. The serpent approached Eve for several reasons, but one in particular was because between the two, Adam and Eve, she was the weaker vessel.

Now weaker in this case means emotional. Eve was the emotional one. Have you notice we as women struggle in our emotions when dealing with others; whereas, the men do not. Now, there is always an exception to the rule.

A woman should first and foremost focus on being a good Christian, and becoming a good wife will be easier. As far as characteristics of a good wife, she should aspire to be a woman of prayer, full of wisdom, virtuous, nurturing, committed to her husband and family, compassionate, loving, kind, having a meek and quiet spirit, capable of showing reverence to her husband, and being faithful unto God. Those are some fundamental characteristics of a good wife. Its important to know that each man will need something different from his wife, but they all will require respect from their wives.

> *Even as Sara obeyed Abraham, calling him lord: whose daughters ye are, as long as ye do well, and are not afraid with any amazement.*
> *1 Peter 3:6 (KJV)*

Women, we must wait on the Lord, if you want to do it God's way. Let's not be like the children of Israel who got so close to the Promised Land. They felt it was hopeless to try to possess the land due to what they called giants in the land, and they saw themselves as grasshoppers. I believe satan wants single Christian women to give up on marriage. I believe satan wants women to become hopeless, as if there are not any more God-fearing men out there to marry.

God instituted marriage, and everything God made was good. On the other hand, satan wants to take God's original plan for marriage and pervert it. Marriage is more than just having someone to have sex with on the regular. I know for myself, I have been asked on several occasion from different people if will I marry again. My answer is yes, I will marry again. I pray that your answer is yes as well, that you will marry. I believe since God ordained marriage between a man and a woman that God is still saying today that it is not good for man to be alone. God will present us, the bride, to our husband in due time. But in the meantime, we need to prepare ourselves for the coming of the bridegroom both naturally and spiritually. So, when the bridegroom comes we will be found ready and not trying to get ready.

> Then shall the kingdom of heaven be likened unto ten virgins, which took their lamps, and went forth to meet the bridegroom. And five of them were wise, and five were foolish. They that were foolish took their lamps and took no oil with them, but the wise took oil in their vessels with their lamps. While the bridegroom tarried, they all slumbered and slept. And at midnight there was a cry made, Behold, the bridegroom cometh; go ye out to meet him. Then all those virgins arose, and trimmed their lamps. And the foolish said unto the wise, Give us of your oil; for our lamps are gone out. But the wise answered, saying. Not so; lest there be not enough for us and you, but go ye rather to them that sell, and buy for yourselves. And while they went to buy, the bridegroom came; and they that were ready went in with him to the marriage: and the door was shut.
> Matthew 25:1–10 (KJV)

Personal scriptures to meditate on:

- Titus 2:3 – The wife is to be in behaviour as becometh holiness, not false accusers, not given to much wine, teachers of good things.

- Titus 2:4 – The older women are to teach the young women to be sober, to love their husbands, to love their children.

- Titus 2:5 – To be discreet, chaste, keepers at home, good, obedient to their own husbands, that the word of God be not blasphemed.

- Proverbs 31:10 – Who can find a virtuous woman? For her price is far above rubies.

- Proverbs 31:11 – The heart of her husband doth safely trust in her, so that he shall have no need of spoil.

- Colossians 3:18 – Wives, submit yourselves unto your own husbands, as it is fit in the Lord.

- Ephesians 5:33b – Wives are to reverence her husband.

- Hebrews 13:4 – Marriage is honourable in all, and the bed undefiled, but whoremongers and adulterers God will judge.

- James 1:17 – Every good gift and every perfect gift is from above, and cometh down from the Father of lights, with whom is no variableness, neither shadow of turning.

- Galatians 3:28 – There is neither Jew nor Greek, there is neither bond nor free, there is neither male nor female: for ye are all one in Christ Jesus.

- Proverbs 14:1 – Every wise woman buildeth her house: but the foolish plucketh it down with her hands.

- James 1:5 – If any of you lack wisdom, let him ask of God, that giveth to all men liberally, and upbraideth not; and it shall be given him.

- 1 Peter 3:1 – Likewise, ye wives, be in subjection to your own husbands; that if any obey not the word, they also may without the word be won by the conversation of the wives.

- Galatians 5:22–23 – But the fruit of the Spirit is love, joy, peace, longsuffering, gentleness, goodness, faith, Meekness, temperance: against such there is no law.

Chapter 10
Role of the Holy Ghost

The Holy Ghost (a.k.a. the Holy Spirit) is the third person of the trinity. The trinity consists of God the Father, God the Son, and God the Holy Ghost. Before Jesus departed from His disciples, He told them that he was going to His Father's house to prepare a place for them. He told them not to be worried because where He was going that they would be there also. He said the way you will know because, "I am the way, the truth, and the life: no man cometh unto the Father, but by me."

He told the disciples that whoever believed in Him and the works that He did, greater works would they do. He also told His disciples anything they asked in His name that He would do. He told his disciples that if they loved Him to keep His commandments. Then He would pray to the Father and He would give them another Comforter that He my abide with them forever. The role of the Holy Ghost is to teach and bring all that Jesus Christ has said back into our minds for remembrance.

> *These things have I spoken unto you, being yet present with you. But the Comforter, which is the Holy Ghost, whom the Father will send in my name, he shall teach you all things, and bring all things to your remembrance, whatsoever I have said unto you.*
> *John 14:25–26 (KJV)*

As our Comforter, He is our teacher, who leads us into all

Truth. The spirit of Truth whom the world did not receive nor knew because the world could not see Him. He told His disciple that they knew Him, and because they knew Him He would dwell with them forever.

> For this is the covenant that I will make with the house
> of Israel after those days, saith the Lord; I will put my
> laws into their mind, and write them in their hearts: and
> I will be to them a God, and they shall be to me a peo-
> ple: And they shall not teach every man his neighbour,
> and every man his brother, saying, Know the Lord: for all
> shall know me, from the least to the greatest.
> Hebrews 8:10–11 (KJV)

As our Comforter, He is our guide and will guide us into all truth:

> I have yet many things to say unto you but ye cannot
> bear them now. Howbeit when he, the Spirit of truth,
> is come, he will guide you into all truth: for he shall not
> speak of himself; but whatsoever he shall hear, that shall
> he speak: and he will shew you things to come.
> John 16:12–13 (KJV)

You may have heard that cord of three strands is not easily broken. Well, in a marriage the Holy Spirit is the third strand that makes the marriage covenant strong. So what God has put together let no man separate.

The Holy Spirit enables the Christian life by dwelling in the individual believer and enables them to live a righteous and faithful life:

> What therefore God hath joined together, let not man put asunder. Mark 10: 9 (KJV)

We can go all the way back to the beginning when God created the heavens and the earth and see the Holy Spirit at work when the Spirit of God moved upon the face of the waters in covenant with God and the Word to create:

> In the beginning God created the heaven and the earth. And the earth was without form, and void; and darkness was upon the face of the deep. And the Spirit of God moved upon the face of the waters. And God said, Let there be light: and there was light.
> Genesis 1:1–3 (KJV)

> "In the beginning was the Word, and the Word was with God, and the Word was God. The same was in the beginning with God. All things were made by him; and without him was not any thing made that was made.
> John 1:1–3 (KJV)

I encourage you to believe that you can create by speaking it into existence. God has given us all the ability to create. Remember we were created in His image and likeness and that He dwells inside of us. Greater is He that is within us than he that is in the world.

Personal scriptures to meditate on:

•   Romans 8:14 – For as many as are led by the Spirit of God, they are the sons of God.

•   Romans 8:15 – For ye have not received the spirit of bondage again to fear; but ye have received the Spirit of adoption, whereby we cry, Abba, Father.

•   Romans 8:16 – The Spirit itself beareth witness with our spirit, that we are the children of God.

•   Romans 8:17 – And if children, then heirs; heirs of God, and joint-heirs with Christ; if so be that we suffer with him, that we may be also glorified together.

•   Acts 2:4 – And they were all filled with the Holy Ghost, and began to speak with other tongues, as the Spirit gave them utterance.

•   Acts 2:39 – For the promise is unto you, and to your children, and to all that are afar off, even as many as the Lord our God shall call.

•   Galatians 3:26 – For ye are all the children of God by faith in Christ Jesus.

•   1 John 3:7 – Little children, let no man deceive you: he that doeth righteousness is righteous, even as he is righteous.

•   1 John 3:9 – Whosoever is born of God doth not commit sin; for his seed remaineth in him: and he cannot sin, because he is born of God.

•   John 1:12 – But as many as received him, to them gave he power to become the sons of God, even to them that believe on his name.

- 1 John 3:1 – Behold, what manner of love the Father hath bestowed upon us, that we should be called the sons of God: therefore the world knoweth us not, because it knew him not.

- Matthew 5:9 – Blessed are the peacemakers: for they shall be called the children of God.

- Ephesians 5:1 – Be ye therefore followers of God, as dear children.

- 1 Peter 2:2–3 – As newborn babes, desire the sincere milk of the word, that ye may grow thereby: if so be ye have tasted that the Lord is gracious.

Notes